The Wonder and
Mystery of Love

The Wonder and Mystery of Love

James Kelly S.J.

The Wonder and Mystery of Love

First published 2002
by
Arderin Publishing Company,
5 Parkview,
Portlaoise,
County Laois,
Republic of Ireland.

ISBN 0 86335 047 X

Cover: Ines Zerbone

DESIGNED AND PRINTED BY LEINSTER LEADER LTD., NAAS.

Contents

To Sister Pius Kelly,
for wonderful support over the years.

Introduction

Since love embraces everything in life, it is impossible to write fully comprehensively about it. Yet the subject is most interesting, since it touches all there that is beautiful, good, enriching, and satisfying. It is mysterious, because in its fullness it is God himself: "God is love" (1 Jn 4.8). And our efforts to understand this marvellous reality, if only in a small way, are attempts to unravel the greatness of the Creator. To view things lovingly in life is to see them with a divine eye.

Life, at its deepest, is a search for love in its wholeness and richness – and so for God. It calls for total openness to him and to draw near to the brightness of his glory, with veneration and respect and with a heart ready to be generously inspired from above. The spiritual person is eager for him and burning with love.

But we all need the warmth of other love. Family and friends are necessary too, in order to keep the homely scene of our living attractive. They can bring us joy and delight – in good and bad times. It is wonderful to give and receive appreciation and approval – causing the feeling or inner core which frequently preserves companionship and friendship!

No doubt all in the world is not love nor sufficiently tinged by it. Hatred, wickedness, and sin are there too. Love tries to change wicked or unpleasant situations, by eliminating evil, or correcting and redirecting what is wrong in a wholesome manner. This task is always possible, even if at times most difficult and slow – thanks to Christ and his redeeming work. Re-patterning erroneous activity with love is a noble, salvific task.

The aim of this writing is to help the reader to open out to the vastness and splendour of love, with a view to sharing in it. It can be enticing and captivating, yet often remains distant and elusive. There is in life the immediacy of human love, with its promises and disappointments, and the serener divine one – less concrete, more controlled and assuring, with its manifold accompanying blessings. True love, however, can seem narrow, cold, and too long drawn out for those seeking quick satisfactions, but given time it shows its brilliance and sureness.

The subject of love is most fascinating and stimulating! Hopefuly, this writing will enable many to increase this quality in their lives, allowing it to blossom in numerous, fruit-bearing ways.

James Kelly, S.J.
Limerick

1

The Charm and Exuberance of Love

From a human point of view, the most satisfying and wonderul thing in life is shared love. It makes living very attractive and even enchanting. Many think that this is something easy and natural – which happens spontaneously and continues on of its own accord. Romantic love is usually of this kind. Two people can fall in love with remarkable rapidity, and giving way to passion can be an equally sudden impulse. Some regard love as mainly a matter of letting things happen or flow, when luck or chance provides a partner. This latter does not always occur.

The feeling of being in love and of being appreciated by another is a powerful boost to the human ego. It means that the inner sensations of a fortunate pair are pulsatingly alive with a type of warm sunshine. There is magic in the contentment they experience. And with such inner delight, their lives move along at a pleasant pace. They can then even endure much, should this be demanded of them for other reasons. Mutual love gives them great support and encouragement, and enlarges their capacity to withstand any discomfort that may arise.

As long as it lasts, the persons so blessed are basically happy. They live in an uplifted marvellous state, knowing that they are most favourably esteemed and valued for their personal grace and worth. They vibrate with joy, peace and trust. Many of them would like to express their delight in poetry and song, conscious that only emotional or artistic literature could convey how they feel. All good art is the fruit of sensed love! "Never durst poet touch a pen to write / Until his ink were temp'red with love's sighs" (Shakespeare).

Reality Not Theory

Much has been written on the subject of love, and all its facets and shades have been dealt with in both serious and trivial ways. But generally speaking, those in love are less concerned about views and discussions on the theme than with the reality itself. They just want to appreciate the blending warmth of their two admiring and sharing personalities, and get as much contentment as they can from shared, generous self-giving. For the time being, they only see the attractive side of each other, with no blemishes or faults alarmingly surfacing. The novelist Moravia wisely remarks: "Love is a glass through which even a monster appears fascinating".

The majority, enlivened by a comforting surrender of the heart, pay little heed to the cautionary wisdom of "the wise and prudent" – being in no way daunted by love's well-known hazards and pitfalls. There may be grave error latent in this, but what matter for the time being! Once embarked on its pleasant path, lovers continue on being attracted by love's soothing melody, until it loses its sweetness and begins to grate – which, alas, eventually may happen.

A pair deeply enamoured like to undertake common activities – going for walks, even on distant holidays, cycling or mountain climbing. They may particularly like to be alone by themselves – "in the clefts of the rock, in the covert of the cliff" (Song 2.14). The urge or longing to be sprightly and free is acutely felt – immortalized in the old song: "Would that we were young and free, the two of us together!".

In Song And Word

A large number of citations from songs and poems on the marvel of love could be given. Love's delight has ever challenged poets to capture its brilliance. Here are just a few:

> "If that girl I could hold, all my raindrops would be gold,
> It would fall all around me, on my Donegal shore". (popular song)

> "Ah, how sweet it is to love!
> And how gay is young desire!
> And what pleasing pains we prove
> When we first approach love's fire!
> Pains of love are sweeter far
> Than all other pleasures are". (John Dryden)

> "Give me a canny hour at e'en,
> My arms around my dearie O,
> An warly cares an' warly men
> Mae all gae tapalteerie O". (Robert Burns)

The German poet Schiller notes what is so eagerly, but in vain, desired: "Would that she remain eternally green, the beautiful time of young love".

He knows how marvellous this is: "O tender longing, sweet hope, the golden time of the first love". But, alas, the years and seasons bring changes, and love, which has the tendency to blossom too soon, is often adversely affected by them. Songs and poetry deal too with such reversals of fortune, usually in a sympathetic and understanding way. Human love is very fickle and unstable, unless pinned down in a stringent and firm manner!

Conviction

Some claim that they have an innate wisdom or sureness, which directs them, as they pursue the enchanted venture of romance. They believe that they have a natural sense or feeling for true love, and that they can recognize the right person for them, as soon as such a one turns up. This belief is in the background, when they say, "We were made for each other" or "Our relationship is very special". They are remarkably trusting in their judgement! The more enlightened are normally sceptical about an intuition of this kind. Still it is part of the charm of love, which sweeps people along!

Uniqueness

There is always an element of mystery in a particular pair being gripped by a strong attraction for each other. It is impossible to unveil all the causes that lead to this or what fully is at stake. The vibrations of affection felt by a pair for one another vary from those experienced by others! If we don't hear or know the inner sighs and cries of their two loving hearts or don't note their nods and winks, we may not realize adequately the drama that is being played out in their lives. We may too easily criticize those who appear to be in love, saying that it's the same old story over again – there being nothing new under the sun! Yet we know that there are always particular and personal aspects to each new friendship or relationship that we make, and that any acquaintance of ours is never fully replaceable by another one. So two lovers ever differ to some degree from any other couple! Thus, there is always something special and singular about a loving relationship, which has to be acknowledged.

Freedom

Genuine love or friendship means giving oneself to another, while at the same time having trusting respect for the other's freedom. Two very devoted and loving people should be able to say: "You are free to be as you wish and have your own friends, just as I have the liberty to do like-wise". Those who unduly stifle the freedom of a friend or lover are limit-ing their worth and spontaneity. Yet a selfish phase normally has to be gone through! Openness to all and largeness of heart may not come easily and may have to be struggled for – overcoming the nasty and curbing strains of possessiveness and jealousy. Love, which is too intensive at the beginning, has usually to be purified and made less exclusive.

Observers, be they relatives or friends or just onlookers, cannot rightly interfere with the choice and the course that lovers take. A pair in love are autonomous and can choose and move forward as they wish, within common limits and subject to the Creator (in the measure that they acknowledge him). They are free to work out how exclusively they stay together – at least for a period! Sufficient space and time have to be given to them, so that they may get to know each other well.

Others need to accept their decisions and adjust to them, as best they can. Whatever their own views, they must respect the rights of the two, to unfold their lives in their own manner. If they think that a pair are erring, they may offer advice, but beyond that, the matter is not their concern. If their suggestions are not welcome, their tolerance may be severely tested – but they can do no more! Lovers are their own masters, within the domain of their love.

Outsiders Wiser!

However, even while bearing in mind all that has been said above, when two people enjoy a wonderful experience of mutual affection, others may rightly view that relationship in a less favourable light. Individuals, well seasoned with the wisdom of years and aware of the deceptions of the heart, may look wryly or with a sense of "déjà vu" at the exaggerations of youthful lovers. If two are very much together and disinterestedly exclude others, those ignored may regard them as too closed and selfish. Of course such criticism may arise from jealousy or from the longings and yearnings of lonely, frustrated hearts.

Nonetheless the observations of others may not be totally wide of the mark. It may be obvious to the sharp observer that there is a prepon-derant element of nervousness or insecurity in a relationship. This may be mainly due to one of the partners, who is either dominating or demanding too much. It may arise too from a fear of losing or that a third party may interfere with the friendship! Possessing or controlling another is a form of violence, and is an attempt to block, free, personal development.

Ever Goes On

Still no matter what opinions people have on the subject of love and its right course, the basic instinct to move along its exquisite track remains embedded in the human person, and nothing is going to quench so powerful a drive. Youth or those young in heart go their own way, as this game of life is ever played. The blending of two personalities in the sway of affection is as old as the hills and keeps on being repeated. The manifestations of mutual esteem by a pair enchanted with and captivated by each other should cause no surprise – since falling in love is one of the sweetest activities of existence, and never loses its appeal.

Just The Beginning

This chapter has dealt only with love in the magical moments of a romantic spell. Viewed against the stretch of a lifetime, such a period may be of short duration! And unfortunately, some individuals may have very scant experience of such a blissful state! Briefly, they find it hard to fall in love.

2

Love at a Less Sure Pace

While for many it's easy to form a special friendship or to start a loving relationship, others find it remarkably hard to win another's heart or to hold on to such a one – even if they are to a degree socially outgoing. As a result, they may frequently ask themselves the belittling question, 'What is wrong with me'? They cannot present themselves to a companion in a way that evokes a reciprocal affectionate response. Their efforts, in this respect, somehow always get twarted. Then after a period of failure, they scarcely believe that they can succeed.

It is possible that there is something wrong in their approach – but it may simply be a matter of bad luck! Some get fixed on a definite person or a few of them, and if they cannot become a particularly good friend of any of these, they feel disappointed and upset. They want their lover to be of a certain kind, someone they have pre-chosen, and they feel incorrect and not content with another who does not conform to what they are looking for. These people generally are too hesitant with a possible partner, because they feel that they have not found the right one – if there be such! The advice is usually given to such seekers or suitors not to be so selective, and not to decide in advance the only type of lover that will satisfy them.

They should let things happen more, and try to develop friendships with those who easily cross their path, and who appeal to some extent to them. They need to be open to new acquaintances, in a calm and interested manner, without being overeager to trap someone as a lover – wanting to get too far, too quickly. Frantic striving in this area tends to end in failure! To succeed in love more flexibility and realism on their part are needed. Instead of a dream companion, someone more ordinary may have to be accepted. And while nature frequently tricks many, so that they see more in the loved one than in fact there is – it can make a crow look like a swan – this does not happen, when individuals are obsessed or blocked by fixed images.

A Too Timid Approach

Undoubtedly some search for a lover in too timid a fashion – being over cautious. They are afraid of getting things wrong or making a bad mistake. They are very, if not excessively, conscious that there are rules and patterns to the swing of love, and that a serious error in this matter would bring them enormous trouble and pain. Perhaps their parents or teachers have deeply driven this fear into them. They want to feel sure where they are going. The wisdom of the old Arabic proverb, whether they know it or not, is embedded in them: "Zeal without knowledge is fire without light".

There is no doubt that many fail on the path of love, and that it is not an easy one. Shakespeare had no illusions about its difficulty, when he wrote: "For to be wise and love exceeds man's might; that dwells with gods above". The words of the same poet that "the course of true love never yet did run smoothly" is a useful reminder of the tensions that are normal in human relationships. These, however, should not be exaggerated, so that people become paralysed, and prevented from trying to make friends. Love may be difficult, but it is far from impossible.

Hard To Preserve

Nevertheless, it is widely acclaimed that love is hard to maintain. Even if a good beginning to it has been made, it may still end up disastrously. Poets have written much about its insecurity – dwelling on its frailty and fickleness. Many would ascribe to this viewpoint. And some, alas, are made over-wary of the dangers of love! Numerous samples could be given, as the following:

"Fain would I love, but that I fear
I quickly would the willow wear;
Fain would I marry, but men say
When love is tied he will away". (R. Hughes)

"Love, in thy youth, fair maid, be wise;
Old Time will make thee colder". (Anon)

"He that loves a rosy cheek
Or a coral lip admires,
Or from star-like eyes doth seek
Fuel to maintain his fires;
As old Time makes these decay, So his flames must waste away".
(T. Carey)

"The flowers do fade, and wanton fields
To wayward winter reckoning yields;
A honey tongue, a heart of gall,
Is fancy's spring, but serious fall". (W. Raleigh)

"Yet remember, midst your wooing,
Love has bliss, a heart of gall,
Other smiles may make you fickle,
Tears for other charms may trickle". (T. Campbell)

Human love is precarious. It has to face up to the four seasons of an emotional year, with an untimely mortality hovering over it. Yet for healthy living, it is well not to dwell too much on the passing beauty of romantic love. Life has to be lived fully, in all its phases, even though it all is leading to a fatal hour and in an earthly sense an end. Happily enough, that fated hour may seem very far away to many people

Disappointment

This may make people very cautious as regards starting a new relationship. Those who have suffered a grim set-back in love know how severe the pain of the heart is – as the Bible so well notes: "The heart knows its own bitterness" (Prov 14.10). "Any wound, but not a wound of the heart" (Sir 25.13). The person who loses a prized friend or lover may personally feel that the whole centre has gone out of life. The situation may be regarded as worse than if a fatality had occurred. Death brings loss, but no sense of being abandoned or thought less of. There is no rejection involved. The individual who suffers an emotional crisis of the heart may be enormously shattered, and it may take a long time to get over this pain. Such a one may have little appetite for the effort involved in a new attempt to acquire another companion. Several failures of this type may leave a person very inhibited.

However some, due to a lack of success too quickly give up, and waste time, bemoaning, in frustration and desolation, their unlucky fate. It would be better for them to keep searching and attempting, rather than to resign themselves to negative feelings!

Loneliness

The repeated failure to attract a lover or friend may cause a frustrated person to become very lonely. It might seem, at first, that this would prove to be an extra spur for making greater efforts to be a winner, but often the contrary is true. The dejected person becomes more withdrawn. This can bring about an unattractive withering of a personality. Such a tendency, if not counteracted, can grow more dominant and crippling with time. Those so suffering find it ever harder to break out of the mould they are in, in order to become more sociable. Unfortunately, too, the lonely, in their isolation, may develop other unhelpful characteristics – be moody or boring, and tending to cling to whoever they find – which are not attractive attitudes. Loneliness is a clear sign that people have to be more outgoing and engaged with life. They need to develop interest in others' concerns and problems – yet this is precisely what they find most difficult to do. Their malaise, terribly gnawing and dulling any zeal and enthusiasm they have, and being like an armoury which confines them too much, militates against moving outwards. In brief, being lonely can shut a person off from searching for a friend, or make such a one vulnerable to a wrong partner – "Any port in a storm". Some, in this condition, grasp even at someone who is unsuitable for them. Their need for love is great, but their pace in searching for it may be either too hesitant or frantic.

Risk Involved

Forming a new friendship or loving relationship always involves risk – who knows what trouble it will bring! But the brave-hearted are not afraid of this. When a pair are strong and calm, they are confident that they will be able to cope with any situation that may arise later! Still there is no way of avoiding the inevitable crises that are certain to follow. Love, even when propelled initially by a warm surge of emotion, takes time to become established deeply and firmly. A pair need a lengthy period of time to get to know each other well – coming to terms with their desires and ambitions, their beliefs and interests, their weaknesses and fears. A slowly developed friendship may be the soundest of all, when a pair over a long period adjust well to each other! Yet before this happens, much can go wrong, and the relationship may never mature. There is no definite pattern in the process of the growth of love, which varies very much.

Many find the risk required too great. They may know too from experience that they are not blessed spontaneously with the correct rhythm for this. They give too much at the beginning or pretend that they are better than they are, and then they can't keep that up. They exaggerate excessively at first, and afterwards have to appear as inferior. Then the other person becomes disappointed, and the esteem previously shown is weakened. Obviously when establishing love or friendship, it is important to be oneself, without falsity or pretence. Sincerity or transparency is a fundamental requisite for establishing true love! A plain, honest approach is called for!

It is, alas, possible to err by over-risking. Quite a few plagued by the fear of rejection and the sad feelings that arise from being alone, want to succeed at all costs. But their unhealthy urgency turns people off. Striving too hard and impatiently can bring about an undesired result – failure to achieve what is wanted. It is possible, as Shakespeare says, to lose by over-running. Those hungry for affection may reach out to several people, yet not alight on anyone sufficiently deeply.

People's futile searches for love and a partner make interesting stories. What some find so natural and easy is a nightmare for others.

The Solution Partly In Oneself

The psychological books are right, when they recommend that we foster in ourselves the traits that we would like to find in a companion. Then we will draw such a one to ourselves! If we are contented and calm, and get on well with people, we will surely attract others who have similar qualities! Becoming a happy and open person is the key to winning friends! Self-contentment is usually rewarded with others' love.

It is important, too, to go where people can be met, in order to form new acquaintances. Initiative means moving to the locations where many congregate. This simply does not mean walking the streets of cities. It rather implies going where a common activity, like sport or walking, is undertaken.

The Imperfect Starting Point

It is a help to the slow and backward in finding companionship or romantic love to realize that the starting point for everyone is imperfect. No two ever begin in an ideal situation, even if their circumstances seem remarkably favourable. What is present at best is the sweet taste or experience of two people gelling well together, but this attraction has to be sustained, developed and worked at, if it is to become permanent. Friendship or love is embarked on in this world as it is, where there are many hazards and upheavals

No two are ever totally suitable for each other. They may have much in common, but their differences are also great. Each has deficiencies and defects, which have to be corrected or they become more acute. Serious mistakes may have been made in the past and opportunities lost, and the same may happen in the future. The negative qualities of parents and teachers have rubbed off on them, and the influence of peers is not always wholesome, and has not been so. The result is that there are lacks and blemishes in every one, which can't be kept for ever dormant. Sooner or later they show up in a love relationship and cause annoyance. It is useful, then, for those who don't succeed in winning a partner, to keep in mind that others, even if they are more fortunate in this, have to struggle too.

A difficulty that frequently arises, in this imperfect scenario, is when one of the partners wants the relationship to become sexually intimate, while the other wishes to abide by a stricter moral code. A failure of the reluctant one to comply with the desires of the other may result in the break-up of their acquaintance. If the conviction of one is very strong that God's law should not be broken, the other may not be willing to accept this. A compromise may be reached, but still the more spiritually minded of the two may be ill at ease. The two have to work out this problem for themselves and it may not be easy. The Almighty's teaching has, as always, to be kept in mind, yet ultimately the consciences of the two have to decide and be satisfied. This often is almost impossible!

Consolation in Being Alone

Some fall in love easily, while others are not so fortunate. There is an element of mystery in it all. Those who don't succeed should realize that God's providence may be protecting them from an unhappy fate! They can draw consolation from the old proverb, "It is better to be alone than in bad company". Fate may be saving them from a harsh destiny!

It is sobering also to bear in mind that there are a big number of people that we meet and may even get to know, yet with whom we would not like to have a close friendship! Being single may free us from being tied to one of these.

It is wise for us to be at ease with our own circumstances in life, whether we are married or not, alone or accompanied. It is somehow all within God's loving guidance or embrace.

The fact that there are a big number of people who don't achieve what they desire, that is win a lifelong partner, is strange. But it is part of the variations and complexity of life.

3

Genuine Self-Love

Psychologists tell us that we cannot adequately love another person or persons, if we don't have sufficient love for ourselves – that is genuine self-love. This latter is a needed requirement for loving others! How this is first acquired as a child is not treated here, where mainly its characteristics are given, though there are indications offered as to how to attain it as an adult and how to foster it. Straightaway, a clear distinction has to be made, since there are two kinds of self-love – one egoistic, the other authentic and liberating. The negative one is an unhealthy concentration on oneself, wanting to receive and to have excessively, without adequate concern about the resulting detriment to other people. This behaviour is selfish, and may spring from a deep dissatisfaction with oneself and one's achievements, and from an accompanying compulsive or pressing need to compensate for what is fundamentally lacking. This leads an individual to be pushy, griping, boastful etc – even ruthless for gain. On the other hand, the person with genuine self-love puts the emphasis on actively loving and accomplishing, in so far as this is conveniently possible, and is a giver and doer more than a receiver or passive.

The need to love oneself is mentioned in the Bible. The second commandment is: "Love your neighbour as yourself" (Mk 12.33). According to this, a person's own self-love should be the standard for loving others. It calls for very personal attention to the neighbour. More biblical texts stress the necessity of loving oneself: "If a man is mean to himself, to whom will he be generous? He will not enjoy his own riches" (Sir 14.5). The individual who is not bounteous towards self is inwardly very paralysed in the matter of love, showing a dismal meanness within.

The burden of not sufficiently esteeming or being contented with oneself manifests itself in observable ways: "Anxiety in a man's heart weighs him down" (Prov 12.25). The NT favours a sounder approach: "Therefore do not be anxious" (Mt 6.31). Warm satisfaction in the heart is noted in the face or countenance: "A glad heart lights up the face" (Prov 15.13). Inner turmoil, on the other hand, saps vitality: "By mental anguish the spirit is broken". A calm attitude is very helpful, while any unease is harmful: "A tranquil mind gives life to the body, but jealousy rots the bones" (Prov 14.30). Even a gloomy book, such as Ecclesiastes, advocates enjoying oneself: "There is nothing better for a man than that he should eat and drink and find enjoyment in his toil. This also, I saw, is from the hand of God" (2.24). "In the days of prosperity be joyful, and in the days of adversity consider: God has made the one as well as the other" (6.14). Yet it is best to aim at happiness: "For if a man lives many years, let him rejoice in them all" (11.8). Being cheerful and contented are signs of true self-love. The advantages of having this are numerous. And so it is not surprising that many people have treated or written on this theme.

Self-love Psychologically Viewed

The abundance of popular psychology books now available on building up self-love and confidence serve a very useful purpose. They set out a pattern or style of living, which it would be good to keep in mind and to quietly follow, as far as is possible. They show or indicate basic attitudes, which both characterize and foster inward strength. They make clear what a strong, healthy and vibrant personality is like.

They call for self-acceptance as a basic requisite. This means warmly appreciating one's own worth, and being at ease with oneself – exactly as one is. It involves recognizing whatever is bad or good in one's make-up. What is there has to be acknowledged – drives, talents, energies, ambitions, achievements, errors, faults, sins. There is no disgust with self, no matter what present conditions or circumstances may be. Being calmly in touch with one's true self, however unbecoming this may be, leaves each in a stronger position than when ignoring partly what is there.

The person with self-confidence is not only relaxed with the present self, but also with what is over and done with. Being so, much turmoil is kept at bay. The errors of the past have to be let go, without harbouring or maintaining a crippling, destructive sense of guilt. What is gone must be accepted in a kind, humble and sanely repentant way. Previous mistakes serve as learning experiences – being blunders which bring or lead to wisdom or better behaviour. The greater they were, the more can be learned from them, and the more possibilities for change and good they provide. That certain things have happened, even what now leads to blushing, show up one's real self! This would not be discovered, if these events did not occur! We would otherwise be suppressing our authenticity! Our errors, properly dealt with, make us richer persons. A stage can be reached in which individuals live comfortably with their former blunders or the wrong directions they have taken – so lessening the belittling, negative feelings that they cause. Wishing matters were different is not only a futile waste of time, but an escape from an individual's existing reality.

The future is viewed with hope and confidence. Anxiety about what lies ahead is considered a useless burden – a galling torment which makes a person less committed to the present and emotionally strained with crippling fears. Life is rather viewed in the perspective of love – for many that is in the light of divine love. The Creator's affection embraces all things, and by means of it his power holds sway. So even if individuals are beset with problems, it is wholesome to trust that their future, directed by love, may be brighter – even if this seems unlikely. Patience and trust in difficulties are other marks of the self-confident person.

Such a one accepts others as they are – respecting their freedom and allowing them to live as they wish. Their virtues are recognized, and their real faults are not ignored. They are not viewed in any prejudicial manner, nor are they set into fixed categories. Scope is left for them to remodel their lives, if they so wish. Their efforts to free themselves from personal limitations and to change are acknowledged and admired.

Psychologists point out more characteristics of those who have adequate self-love. They tend to be filled with energy and enthusiasm, if their circumstances are in any way favourable to them. They are eager to achieve what they can, and are not afraid of taking risks. They have the freedom to give of their best. They can express their feelings easily enough, and don't timidly suppress them. Part of their strength comes from the way in which they make use of their emotions for good. They radiate self-assurance and goodwill. They are warmly loving and tend to be loved by others. Their confident attitude evokes warm responses from those whom they meet.

Growth In Self-love

Popular psychological books, usually written for adults, also aim at helping individuals to correct their deficiencies and personal defects. Yet what they recommend may seem beyond the capacity of groping, confused individuals, who are unable to cope with the complete change of attitudes, that are recommended. A new and better life-orientation cannot be achieved rapidly. But in fact, these writings realistically suggest that small constructive steps be taken each day, while moving in a forward direction. They favour positive thinking, active love and repeating affirmations. They want all to start and to keep growing as assured and loving people.

It may take considerable time for some to realize that there are deficiencies in their personality, and even longer to convince them that they ought to try to improve. Yet the need to do so is real for quite a few. Many grow up with a negative self-image, and are far less assured and confident than they should be. There are as well those who have developed a false personality, which belies their true selves, and they should try to change this. But there are lesser strains. The majority are burdened with unruly feelings, anger, envy, a sense of guilt or a feeling of failure – all of which limit their present well-being! Even this awareness is a step forward. A healthier and saner outlook can always be developed. Still it may not be easy to undo the damage caused in the past, but a great deal can be done!

A child that is born into a healthy, secure and supporting family is given a great start, as regards self-appreciation and self-confidence. Others less fortunate in their birth often don't have as smooth a passage in this regard. But some of them may find a kind helper or benefactor early in life – an inspiring teacher or a coach – who compensates for what is lacking, by personally building them up and bringing the best out of them. These, too, are lucky.

Loving Others

Self-love is not developed in isolation from others. Maturity is only arrived at, by being engaged with neighbours and responding fittingly to them. Yet the basic psychological tenet, already referred to, is most relevant and needs to be borne in mind, namely that to love others, we have to be at ease with ourselves. Otherwise we don't have the freedom, trust and assurance to give ourselves constructively to them, and to risk wisely the venture of friendship or love. From a personally secure position, we are more likely to give more than we receive, and to be truly outward going rather than inward looking!

It is a useful exercise to read passages from some of these popular psychological books, in order to be reminded of what we can do to improve our personalities. The steps we take are best done with or under a religious vision! The balanced person is psychologically, intellectually (as far as is needed), and spiritually strong – capable of loving self, God and others!

Caution Needed

All that has been written so far about the positive side of living has to be viewed as relative, and treated with care. Not all are blessed with the vision and attitudes called for. Many grow up in situations which make the attaining of these difficult. Their outlook on reality may be less optimistic than others would like them to have. And yet in many things the negative is as true as the positive – something may be half empty or half full.

We need to be very cautious in assessing people's negativity, as Romano Guardini has pointed out. Sometimes these have a deeper

intuition than others into what is good and beautiful and they are profoundly disappointed with whatever does not measure up to what they
would like. Perhaps they have set higher standards in all too. They may be
sharper than others at assessing matters, even if their viewpoints cause
them to be considered as being too critical. The divine directive not to
judge others ever holds sway. Positive thinkers may be overeager for
things to be seen in a certain way!

Psychologically Sound Not All

It would be wrong to think that psychological ease or so-called normality
is everything that is needed to face life wisely. This does not solve the full
range of human needs – as for example, that of poverty. Each person has
other, even nobler requirements. It is evident that individuals may be
sound psychologically, but may have other difficulties such as spiritual
blindness. Even their psychological strength may work against them. The
security it brings can dispose them to go astray, in other ways. It doesn't,
in fact, mainly determine how they will turn out. It has to be recognized
that a higher plan governs all lives, be it fate of some kind or for the
Christian believer, God's providence. This may bring about great success
or dire tragedy, or a variety of mixed situations in between. The Creator
can always change enormously the state or circumstance of any individual, as von Balthasar has indicated: "God not only finishes his own word
of creation, but also takes as well the no of man and fashions out of it his
own and man's yes". Even though individuals grow up in harsh, social settings, religion and God's guidance may orientate them wholesomely
towards sound living. God's grace works on people's psychological make-
up, and often brings about needed corrections or counterbalances there. It
is important above all not to forget that to accept Christ and his message
and to follow him, show a very positive attitude towards life.

Psychological soundness has to fit into a pattern of sublimer values and
contribute to the attaining of other goals – such as spiritual ones. It is very
important, and is a dimension of life that should never be ignored. In the
past, religious teaching tended to overlook this domain, and to build on
top of psychological defects, with a far from happy result. Yet getting the
balance right is difficult.

It is best when the psychological and spiritual dimensions of a person
work hand in hand. Efforts made on the natural plane help people to be
more humanly alive and active, but this needs to be just part of a fuller
system. A huge factor in life is God's grace. With this, the Almighty can
adorn a personality, even in very strange ways, and can use psychological
lacks to his own advantage.

4

Basic Structures and Achievements of Love

The basic pattern of behaviour of two people who fall in love has already been dealt with. A more permanent structure is arrived at, when a family is formed. This is something impressively beautiful, at least when it works well and holds cohesively together. When parents and children live, in general, in harmony (minor tensions are inevitable), a warm atmosphere radiates in the home and from there. This usually presumes that an adequate income is coming in each week, as excessive poverty may make life unbearable, and cause crippling strain. Yet a relatively poor family may be a happy one, at times even a very poor one!

The Bible gives us some indications as to what brings about a contented marriage. The role of parents is paramount, even if difficult. "Fathers, do not provoke your children to anger, but bring them up in the discipline and instruction of the Lord" (Eph 6.4). They ought not to be aggressive with their offspring, but kind to them. They above all have the duty to teach them to respect God and obey him. Theirs is a very honourable task given to them by the Creator (cf Sir 3.2).

Sons and daughters have to play their part too – recognizing respectfully their parents as their masters. "Children, obey your parents in the Lord, for this is right. 'Honour your father and mother'" (Eph 6.1,2). The need to do this has to be impressed greatly on young people. This, however, always presumes that the couple are playing their part well. Many blessings result from such esteem from the younger generation: atonement for sin, riches, joy in one's own children, one's prayer is heard, a long life (cf Sir 3.3-6). The blessings that follow a warm attitude towards parents are enormous. The Lord is most generously disposed towards those who keep this command: "Honour your father by word and deed, that his blessing may come on you" (Sir 3.8).

A Good Wife

Scripture glowingly praises a good wife. And what is said about her surely has to apply to some extent to the husband too! A capable bride is hard to find – which may be a negative starting point. The majority, then, have to be content with someone less wonderful, and must be prepared for this! She is very precious. She inspires trust, works and does good to her man all his life – divorce, then, is not acceptable! (cf Prov 31.10-13). She brings joy to him, and, as a result, he will complete his years in peace (Sir 26.2). She lengthens his days (Sir 26.1), since she makes his heart tranquil. No matter what their circumstances, she brightens his existence: "Whether rich or poor, his heart is content, and at all times his face is cheerful" (Sir 26.4). A good wife is wise, yet speaks with tenderness (Prov 31.26). She is strong and dignified (Prov 31.25). She is an adorning, towering figure in the home: "Like the sun rising in the heights of the Lord, so is the beauty of a good wife in her well-ordered home" (Sir 26.16). She is like a shining lamp (Sir 26.17) – exuding brightness. Not all wives come up to this high standard! It is worth noting the importance the Bible gives to the role of the wife in the family. One wonders if this has to be so in all happy matrimonial unions! It is useful for a couple to keep the instructive observations mentioned here in mind. The truth is that many marriage situations don't shine so brightly. Yet being aware of what should be there is itself helpful. Husbands and wives are considered blessed in the Bible, and greatly assisted by it.

The beauty and goodness of a marital union is, in general, evident when the members of a family convey joyful esteem and work for each other, share delights and sorrows, struggle together in the face of difficulties, and calmly accept what cannot be avoided. It is particularly noticeable on certain occasions. The depth and generosity of family love are very much to the fore, when a father and mother visit a sick or troubled child, in hospital or in prison, or write or telephone to a distant son or daughter. Its courage is serenely present, when the harsh blows of fortune are calmly and responsibly faced up to. Loyalty to a close relative in disgrace shows how thorough and kind family support is. Its frailty and nobility are given expression, when a painful bereavement strikes. Its magnanimity gives freedom to sons and daughters to go their own way and develop as they wish, even though restraining and disagreeing advice may have to be given. A family is exposed to mishaps and suffering on many fronts – far more than a single person! It demands by its very nature charitable living.

Viewed at its profoundest, it is a reflection of the Blessed Trinity. The Father generates the Son from all eternity, and both bring forth the Holy Spirit. Husband, wife and children are a symbol of the triune God, even if a pale one. Their mutual respect and love, their sharing of ideas and interests, and their constructive work together, bear an important similarity to the divine life – something mysterious. The real value of a marital union, as of every individual life, is the extent to which divine glory adorns it. The humblest of marriages, in the poorest of circumstances, may shine very brightly to the divine eyes.

This relationship is viewed another way in the NT, with a more particular emphasis on Jesus. A pair live out, as far as they can, the mystery of Christ's relationship with his Church. "Husbands, love your wives, as Christ loved the church and gave himself up for her, that he might sanctify her" (Eph 5.25, 26). All lasting marriages share in the mystery of Jesus' faithful love, something very wonderful.

Friends

The worth of a good friend cannot easily be overestimated! All of us are indebted to such people, who have proved their loyalty to us. These, most likely, are only a few, since genuine friendship is rare! We all have experience of abortive attempts to find worthwhile companions, but which somehow did not work out. A good friend is one in a thousand, according to the Bible (Eccles 7.28).

This divinely inspired writing knows how precious these supports are. "Faithful friends are a sturdy shelter; whoever finds one has found a treasure. They are beyond price; no amount can balance their worth. They are life-saving medicine" (Sir 6.14-16). They are a marvellous assistance, protect us, and give us vitality. A true friend is helpfully at hand in times of difficulty or need (Sir 37,4,5) – as an old, seemingly universal proverb states. The person who vanishes, when life gets tough for another, lacks the real core that should mark friendship, namely being always with and offering fitting support. Friendship, however, goes too far, when dubious or unjust favours are given to a friend!

A companion of such a genuine calibre has to be carefully preserved. The Bible, in this regard, stresses above all the need to be confidential. Once this is broken, the required mutual goodwill is badly shattered. "Whoever betrays secrets destroys confidence, and will never find a congenial friend. Love your friend and keep faith with him; but if you betray his secrets, do not follow after him … so you have killed the friendship of your neighbour" (Sir 27.16-18). Being tight-lipped especially about another's hidden behaviour, if one happens to know it, is due out of reverence to the person concerned. Any unnecessary breach of this is betrayal – usually very serious.

It is fitting for us to recall frequently, in a thankful way, those who are or have been our friends. They may have boosted and comforted us, when we had to face disappointment or when we were worried, and enabled us to view matters in a brighter, more hopeful perspective. They, perhaps, brought joy to us in sadness, and restored our trust and confidence, when these seemed to have deserted us. They may have encouraged us to be patient and to look elsewhere, in the face of others' hostile behaviour towards us. They may have urged us on to undertake new ventures, convincing us that they were worth the effort and risk. It is a pleasant exercise to muse on how friends have helped us. Briefly, they steadied our ship, when we were floundering. They may not have been able to help us much financially, though perhaps a little. But, in general, they have been greatly beneficial to us. We could trust them, and work out our own ideas with them.

The Achievements Of Love

It would be hard to do adequate justice to this second part. Everything constructive that has taken place, or is being accomplished, is the fruit of love, while all that is negative springs from its lack or misuse. Each of us has some knowledge of what it achieves – and so of its might. Yet we have only limited awareness of the vastness and extent of all that is done under the sun. We mainly know what touches us in the small world in which we live. This writing refers to a small portion of what springs from the creativity of individuals or from the harmonious working and cooperation of many hands together

We are impressed, at times, by the music of a soloist of any kind, such as a singer, which fills our ears with delightful sounds. We know that this is the expression of a warm-hearted soul. Be it mellifluous operatic or melancholy traditional, we are moved by the loving vibrations of the artist who performs, and by the composer.

A splendid production of an opera, to which many skilled people contribute, singers, instrumental musicians, lighting experts, stage directors, sponsors, organizers, is a marvellous example of what a group working in unison can bring about. It's like a cruise liner putting out to sea. But there are lesser, yet very noble, accomplishments. A simple presentation of a play, in a rural town or village, shows goodwill, a community effort, and shared loving interest. The voices and acting talents of locals, who freely give of their best, evoke in us a homely appreciation of simple goodness. The depth of love behind such success is not ours to judge.

When two or more work at a project, the result is usually visible – like a wall or house built, a garden sown, a book produced, a film, a game played, something made. Labour of all kinds, for the most part, brings about what is beneficial to humanity. (War and arms are sorry exceptions). The thrill and exuberance of sport enliven many a heart – the exertions of the players causing this. We may know very little about art, but a harmony of colours lifts our spirits. A painting of a lovely landscape, such as a vividly green Irish scene (like Croghan Hill) may stay in our imaginations for years, and evoke now and again the memory of a youthful impression that abides hopefully for ever.

What love is expressed in countless books – in poetry, dramas of all kinds, novels and stories! Most of us have come in contact with a certain amount of this richness, even if our acquaintance with the oceanity of world literature is very limited. Very few can cope well with its vastness – only those with a touch of genius! Yet the small portion of it that impinges on our lives widens our sympathies for others, and enables us to be more sensitive towards their uniqueness and peculiarities, and to be more magnanimous in esteeming their worth.

An enlightened novel or life-story could be written about everyone! It could be best done by the individual concerned, should such a one be able to give vent to the sensitivities felt within, by possessing the writing skill needed! Yet not all are able to put into words the joys and sorrows, the lights and shades, the successes and failures, the twists and turns, the strange and personal happenings and experiences which they have lived through, in the span of an existence. It is impossible for an outsider to grasp all that goes on in another's life – unless such a one's self-revelation brings it to the fore! A drama of depth and originality may remain hidden there, unseen by gazing eyes. The emotional struggle of another may be very remarkable, and portray a grandeur more than acquaintances realize. Such a one may have a heart "pregnant with celestial fire", but it all remains unknown. Reverence for one's neighbour is ever needed.

The more mundane scientific progress in all its many facets – visible to a degree in any big city or store – is, in part, the fruit of altruistic love! It is brought about by those who want, to some degree, to make life easier and better for others – though other motives may be far more dominant.

Gratitude

The achievements of love are enormous and they impress us every day. They call for appreciation and gratitude from us – qualities that we can never have over-abundantly. It is likely that we don't thank our ancestors enough for all their toil and for what they have handed down to us. We have been plunged, happily enough, into a world vastly developed – with much on offer, due to the skills and labours of those who have gone before us.

Our best way of showing thanks is not only to admire and to praise, but to be part of the same accomplishing. This brief focussing on the extensive panorama of the fruits of love serves as an invitation to us, to engage in similar activity – to be up and doing, loving and helpful. We should at least play a tiny part in it!

5

Tragedies And Failures In Love

It is very commonly known that loving relations often don't run smoothly. Those once passionately in love with each other and who thought life would be impossible, if they were separated, can become cruel and bitter enemies – as vicious dislike, anger, resentment, and bitterness mount up. A pair, whose emotions formerly seemed glued to one another, can drift and be severed apart – with their mutual affection and personal understanding fading or declining. As a result, many are led to ask: Why does love change so drastically? Why can it turn so sour? The corruption of love is terrible. And a more fundamental question arises: Is human love ever secure? The conclusion, then, is reached by some that there is no such thing as eternal love.

Tragedies

Murder can happen because of deep emotions gone wrong. Tragedies of a horrific and vengeful kind, both real and on stage, sometimes portray the fury that is generated by the decline or collapse of love, as it generates into a wild, destructive force. When a once bright source of happiness and joy loses its gripping appeal, life may become a harsh nightmare for a bewildered and disorientated person. The resulting sense of disappointment and failure can be so profoundly felt, that it leads an individual to take drastic measures. Such serious and grim tragic happenings do occur, striking both young and old. The extreme and mad solution to take one's own life or to remove another by killing may seem to be the only way out of a torturous existence – but it is always cowardly and erroneous! The fallacy of trying to better oneself by doing wrong always misfires. And still, however appalling or atrocious a wayward course of action may be, it ever remains within the mystery of love. Such incidents cause heart-rending anguish, even if they quietly evoke great human sympathy from those aware of them.

However meaningful and strangely uplifting that folly may be in the embrace of divine Providence, as observers and thinkers like von

Balthasar have pointed out – "What makes life profound and noble, if not suffering and tragedy?" – its immediate reality, is horrifying and painful. Normally, failed love causes less distress – just dull rumblings of discontent, anger, and quarrelling. This latter turmoil, however, can be somewhat alleviated by the support of other people and friends, but it can persist for a long time, as a form of mild torment.

It would be wrong to pass an ultimate judgement on those who choose a tragic solution. Greek drama dealt with such events, not only describing their sequence in detail, but offering an explanation as to what lay behind them. The gods or Providence, according to Greek thinkers, tied people up in unsatisfactory situations, and these, in their efforts to free themselves, often pulled the wrong strings – with dire results. King Oedipus laments that his good conscience led him astray, when unknowingly he killed his father and married his mother. He states his position clearly: "As regards me, how can it be believed that my disposition was bad, if all I had done was to react to offences. … But I have arrived where I have arrived, not conscious of anything. Those who made me a victim know certainly how to destroy me" (Oedipus At Colonus). He is aware that his life at a profound level was planned by another, and that his decisions were being directed by a more general plan. The words of the prophet, Jeremiah, come to mind: "I know, O Lord, that the way of man is not in himself,/ that it is not in man who walks to direct himself" (10.23).

But tragic events proved more puzzling and mysterious for another Greek playwright. Euripides failed to see why any individual would choose such a way? He recognized, nonetheless, that the nobility and generosity of those who undertake voluntary suffering and death for others are admirable. He sensed the grandeur in it, but he could not grasp fully what constituted its greatness.

It is rather harsh to look on tragedy in a judgemental way, viewing it as a punishment for wickedness. The confused motives of those directly involved in a tragic act and the pressures on them from outside may be enormous, and not totally knowable. All this serves as a warning to us to respect and be kind in our thinking towards them. The Christian wisely entrusts their fate to the loving and superabundant mercy of God.

Love Changing

When two people grow very close with blending feelings and even pledge the durability of their warmly felt esteem, such harmony and goodwill does not always last. Human affection is like a colour that far too easily fades. Love, at first, is a magic light, that solely brings up the attractive qualities in the other person. With time the less pleasant sides come to the fore.

The sparkle of the eyes, the softness and clearness of skin, the fresh appearance, and the inward glow, which strike winningly a lover, at the initial stages, eventually lose their intensity. Much more so, this happens with the passing of years, due to the continual drudgery of daily living (the struggle to survive), and to health problems – all causing ugly bodily contours to develop. Familiarity causes a pair to become tired and weary of one another. Worse still, their peculiarities grate and prove annoying.

Love calls for sharing – which is very difficult for the egoist. The individual who wants all or most is turned inwardly too much and is not adequately open to consider the needs of the other. Self is too important for such a person. Egoism destroys many marriages.

In general, human love promises more than it delivers. Shakespeare has masterly described this fact: "This is the monstrosity in love, lady – that the will is infinite and the execution confined; that the desire is boundless and the act a slave to limit. … They say all lovers swear more performance than they are able … vowing more than the perfection of ten, and discharging less than the tenth part of it". In the same play, the importance of intellectual growth, to preserve love, is stressed – "Outliving beauties outward, with a mind / that doth renew itself swifter than blood decays". Spiritual development, too, can give a very solid dimension to love, and has a vital contribution to make to preserving it.

The realistic conclusion has to be reached that love cannot be sustained by outward looks or emotional satisfaction, but needs something stronger and inwardly more gripping, in order to grow and survive.

The Great Variety Of People

The second enemy of love arises from the richness of the world – from the great variation of characters in it. No matter how satisfied an individual may be with a loved one, someone else more attractive is bound sooner or later to show up, making the old heart-enchanter look at least a second best. The appeal of a new person may dampen that of an old companion – putting it in the shade. The newly arrived may be more handsome or wealthier, have more talents and success, be renowned in some way, and have a more winning disposition. Under the spell of the new vibrations of love, feelings that were considered dormant may arise once more, and old dreams, whether repressed or forgotten, may want to be lived out. Some under the pressure of a recently discovered charm are swept off their feet and plunge into another amorous adventure – which may not work so well! Goethe describes the passion and perhaps folly of the new commitment: "To you I pledge my strength, my whole desire, / Passion's quintessence, all the fire, / The idolatry, the madness of my heart".

The ever abiding temptation to be a Don Juan is very real. Why stay with one lover, when there are so many available? Why not avail of the abundance that life offers and share more in the world's fullness – if only for a time! The same German poet is aware of the restlessness that follows the taste of love: "Human life / Is various, various are the hours of men. The lover may embrace what he desires, / But longs at once for something still more sweet". Human love is never totally fulfilling. There are limitations to the Don Juan approach. At most, it is only possible to have a relatively small number of lovers, out of all that might be. The vast majority can't be reached by any individual. Furthermore, the person who frequently changes partner lives only on the surface of love and never knows its depths! Once the affections are scattered too widely, they don't impinge sufficiently on anyone, to give the type of joy that the human spirit seeks! When there is too much searching for new companions in life, peace and contentment are impossible; for endless struggle and infuriating craving are mainly dominant

We all have to learn that true love comes more from within ourselves than from without – from finding our own inner strength, even if that is a gift from above. Inner peace can always be found, in any situation, whether one be married or single! It is not arrived at by chasing after people! The Don Juans of the world don't really love anyone, not even themselves!

Economic Problems And Sickness

Other enemies of love are financial problems and ill health – yet not always so. There are wonderfully happy relationships among the poor, and the precarious health of a partner may bring out remarkable tenderness and generosity in the other. Whether these situations are exceptional or not is difficult to say. In view of this, the following observations have to be treated cautiously, and not be generalized.

If monetary pressures are acutely burdensome, making mere survival a nightmare, a calm, attentive relationship among lovers is hard to maintain. The struggles of the poor, bringing on strain and tiredness, make them irritable, nervy, and without the energy to be flexible! They, then, may not have the ease and strength, to refine their personal and social skills especially on the domestic front. The biggest factor causing the breakup of marriages is considered to be the economic one! Yet a moderate degree of poverty may contribute to increasing the depth of love between people – and may well be a useful stimulus for them to cooperate better together.

The bad health of a family member causes distress, extra work, inconvenience and expense, and may demand great sacrifice from the others. In such a situation, being always patient and gentle may not be easy. When

combined with poverty or other contrary matters, sickness makes it hard
to maintain the serenity of love, and may lead to quarrelling. Yet there are
cases, and they may be quite numerous, where illness ennobles a family.

It is, however, always a blessing, when accepted in the right spirit. It is
a trial which tests the genuineness and depth of love. But it can sanctify
people greatly. Its strange beauty is evident, when it somehow opens people to love more. For this to happen, help is needed from on high! There
is no situation where love cannot win out.

Riches

Wealth, too, in its own peculiar way can be an obstacle to love. Too much
concern for it makes individuals hard and tough – and so without the sensitivity and kindness that go with tender affection! If riches are too
esteemed, they become an idol. The person who excessively sets the heart
on them develops like them, materialistic, hard and insensitive – as the
Bible rightly says: "Their makers (of idols) shall be like them, everyone
who trusts in them" (Ps 115.8).

Furthermore, extra lovers or friends can be bought with money – something which interferes with the flow of natural friendship. Money also, as
Scripture says, facilitates sin. "The lover of gold will not be free from sin,/
for he who pursues wealth is led astray by it" (Sir 31.5).

Changes of fortune, especially from good to bad or from riches to
poverty, ruin many a friendship or relationship! The old wisdom, which is
expressed in the Bible, is taught by life to many: "There is a friend who will
be with you, while you are contented, but in times of trouble he stands afar
off" (Sir 37.4). Most so-called friends quickly vanish, when things go badly
for us. A genuine one is supportive in good and bad times. Worldly people
only stay with the successful. Shakespeare was aware how a person's life
changes with a reversal of fortune. "This world is not for aye(ever), nor 'tis
not strange that our lives should with our fortunes change".

Jealousy And Being Unable To Pardon

The Bible knows how vicious jealousy can be: "Jealousy is as cruel as the
grave" (Song 6.6). It can lead people very far astray. It is a mean and
demeaning vice – showing a lack of magnanimity and respect for others –
not recognizing their gifts. At first, it might seem to be an ally of faithful
love, causing a pair to show extra interest in each other. But it may do so
too much, to the exclusion of other people. Jealousy or envy, desirous of
keeping a third party at bay, may lead to one person trying to prevent
another from cultivating friends. Striving to possess a person completely is

never correct. This defect, which is partly due to an inferiority complex or a lack of self-esteem, is at variance with the ease and freedom that should mark true love. Connected with this defect is another one – being unable to forgive. Since all are imperfect, and errors, even serious ones, can never be excluded, the fidelity of true love may demand pardoning or forgiving.

Death And Separation

Not only time and the changes it brings can be enemies of love. But these are also a preparation for a more radical foe. Death is the most powerful factor arrayed against human love. With its merciless onslaught, it breaks up partnerships. It removes one of the friends or lovers beyond the reach of sight and ordinary speech. In a worldly sense, it totally destroys the bonds of a lifetime. However, it has to be viewed spiritually – which puts it in a totally new light. It is hostile to love only in a human sense.

Apart from death, there are other separations in life. Even the best of friends may have to live far apart – due to circumstances, such as work. When two people are distanced and don't see each other and directly exchange views, it is difficult for them to keep their friendship warmly alive, unless it has been previously very well established. Some develop familiarity with others through letter writing, but this is more an intellectual relationship than one based on personal attraction!

Other friends are lost due to the swings and blows of life. Its hazards cause people to separate, and so they don't meet each other. Their previous friendship probably does not die, but may live on in memories, well-wishing and dreams.

Life demands that many go their own ways and forget old acquaintances. This is natural, as friendships often are not deeply established, nor destined to last. Time and place bring about many losses. But, in fact, these may be blessings, being a deliverance for two people, who would not be good for each other!

*   *   *   *

The frailty of human love causes people to wonder if there is such a thing as eternal love – a fact already mentioned. All rightly sense, at times, that the deepest yearnings of the heart cannot be satisfied by a human person or persons, even if they would like this to happen! Fortunately a higher love has been made known to and shared with us – that of God. We are all, if in varying degrees, within the power and radiance of his love. That same is ever creative, constructive and embellishing. How deeply it impinges on us has to be seen. It is the richest love that can be encountered – surpassing, wonderful and mysterious.

6

God's Love Revealed In The Old Testament

The Bible reveals a God of love to us. This has as its starting point the fact that he is the Creator – the One who shares. He is the great and most generous giver. Without him we would not be alive, nor kept in existence. But he goes even further, both forming and protecting us.

Creation

All that the Lord has made or makes is underpinned by his love. "Who alone does great wonders, for his steadfast love endures forever … who spread out the earth upon the waters, for his steadfast love endures forever" (Ps 136.4,6). This devout person, very aware of what the Almighty has done, recognizes this with praise and thanksgiving: "For thou art great and doest wondrous things, thou alone art God. … I will give thanks to thee, O Lord, my God, with my whole heart" (Ps 86.10,12). His deeds should be vividly kept in mind. "Bless the Lord, O my soul, and forget not all his benefits" Ps 103.2). The earth is filled with his blessings (Sir 16.27). His largesse can be viewed also in terms of goodness. Everything the Lord made was good (Gen 1. 25).

Man and woman are the jewels of his creative activity. The Almighty was most satisfied after he had made them: "And indeed, it was very good" (Gen 1.31). Each person is formed in his image and likeness. There are various explanations given as to what this means. The Bible nowhere clarifies the matter. For Gregory of Nyssa it is a participation in the infinite goodness of God. St John of Damascene sees it in the unfathomable mystery that man and woman were created for deification – and are moving towards union with him. In general, the image of God refers to the whole human make-up – to the entire person. It is the tendency in each to be fully united with the Creator! This characteristic in every person has always to be respected with reverence, no matter how degenerate an individual may be. Such a divine imprint is never totally destroyed by wickedness, and can ever be revitalized and brightened.

In the beginning, the first pair had direct contact with the Almighty. They had companionship and open dialogue with him. "Their eyes saw his glorious majesty, and their ears heard the glory of his voice" (Sir 17.11). They were loved and inspired by him: "He looks with favour upon their hearts, and shows them his glorious works" (Sir 17.7). They in turn were to acknowledge what he had done and praise him (Sir 17.8). Their task was to multiply and to rule over all creation – both divinely given roles. "Be fertile and multiply; fill the earth and subdue it" (Gen 1.28). They needed to obey him, in order to accept and recognize him as their Master. Alas, Adam and Eve failed in a serious manner to do precisely this: they were disobedient – thus bringing sin into their lives and the world. One can't just sin and only affect oneself. There is no such thing as an isolated sin. Evil, alas, spreads very rapidly. The mystery of iniquity is something we must ever try to understand more fully. The failure of the first parents happened long ago, yet it still affects us.

Sin And Promise

God did not abandon humanity, when the first pair went beyond the limits that he set for them and got entangled in their own wickedness. He then revealed himself not only as their Creator and Sustainer, but also as their Saviour. He made known a kindness, which later was described in this way: "The Lord is merciful and gracious, slow to anger and abounding in steadfast love. ... He does not deal with us according to our sins, ... as far as the east is from the west, so far he removes our transgressions from us" (Cf Ps 103. 8-14). God's love, happily for us sinners, is one that always pardons. He immediately promised a redeemer or saviour – being in no way caught off guard by what happened. This gave rise to the hope of an eventual, total solution to the problem of evil – a comforting light for all struggling individuals.

The Lord's fidelity to his creatures still held firm, when he was angry that their sinfulness was rampant, as they had gone wild. "The Lord saw that the wickedness of mankind was great on the earth, and that every inclination of the thoughts of their hearts was only evil continually" (Gen 6.5). When the Almighty decided that such negativity had to be curbed and that he had to take drastic, punitive measures, he still remained, if in a limited sense, a Saviour. God said: "I will blot out from the earth the human beings I have created – people together with animals and creeping things and birds of the air, for I am sorry that I have made them" (Gen 6.7). But a small, yet significant group, were protected, namely Noah and his household.

A Special Vocation

A long time elapsed, before God intervened again in a remarkable manner. How great is his patience, how slow his interfering, how carefully worked out his plans and timing! The greatness and mystery of God is evident in all of these. He called Abraham and through him set in motion a vast undertaking: "Go from your country and your kindred and your father's house to the land that I will show you. I will make of you a great nation, and I will bless you, and make your name great, so that you will be a blessing" (Gen 12.2). The patriarch did not know all that was involved in this command – much less what would result from it. But he went as he was directed. He undertook a long and insecure journey.

As the story is read now, he was inspired by the Almighty's call and promise. He must have relied heavily on this to keep him going. Frequently, then, he heard the Lord's voice echoing in his ears and, as a result, felt the assurance that he was on the right track! He was guided by the spiritual light that issued from the divine words – the plan or word of the Almighty made known to him. But all did not happen over night – the designs of the Creator often take place slowly. Abraham, no doubt, at times felt weary and perplexed, even tempted to turn backwards, but he kept going forward, trusting in God's word, while not knowing where his final destination lay (Heb 11.8). He was a man guided by faith and hope. God caused him to embark on a long journey, to live a migratory existence, moving onwards to an unknown goal. The NT regards him as the model of a believer: "By faith Abraham obeyed when he was called to go out to a place which he was to receive as an inheritance; and he went out not knowing where he was to go" (Heb 11.9). The life of faith is a similar journey.

How far he was conscious of his vocation and the significance of his movements is another matter. It is possible that the happenings of his life were only interpreted religiously later! Many, in fact, achieve more than they realize, and, perhaps Abraham was one of them! It may have been his descendants who long afterwards realized the importance of his calling and its profounder implications – leading to a divine covenant (agreement) with humanity, based on mutual fidelity (Gen 17.1-14). Whether this be so or not, Abraham must have been an impressive figure. His memory lived on as the leader of a group, who travelled far in response to a divine voice. He knew to some extent that God was with him. Later generations were able to interpret it all more profoundly!

The vocation given to Abraham was the first of what are now known as special ones. The Almighty selects people for a definite and particular task, and asks them to serve him in the way he indicates and in view of what he promises – as in the NT, when Jesus said: "Come behind me, and

I will make you fishers of men (women)" (Mk 1.17). It involves moving from one position and going towards another – whether this be viewed spatially or qualitatively. The chosen person's old way of life has to be left behind, and a new one undertaken. A radical change of lifestyle frequently is demanded – one that calls for great readiness. A strong conviction that to obey is worthwhile is needed too.

Liberation

God's fidelity to his word given to Abraham was again most remarkably evident, when he came to the rescue of the patriarchs' descendants who were enslaved in Egypt. These had fallen into a very adverse situation – something which did not escape the notice of the Creator. He was aware of their pain, heard their pleas for help, and was determined to help them: "I have observed the misery of my people who are in Egypt; I have heard their cry on account of their taskmasters. Indeed, I know their sufferings, and I have come down to deliver them out of the hand of the Egyptians, and to bring them up out of that land to a good and broad land, a land flowing with milk and honey" (Ex 3.7-8). He saw, heard, and knew that something had to be done, and he began to act. He planned to rescue them, under the leadership of Moses, and to give them a new homeland, where they could fittingly worship him. (Yet such deliverance involved the destruction of another people, the Canaanites! – the ways of God are strange). His callings and gifts have a spiritual purpose. Adoring the Almighty in the right setting was demanded – and was the main motive for the Exodus! "The God of the Hebrews has revealed himself to us; let us go a three day's journey into the wilderness to sacrifice to the Lord our God, or he will fall upon us with pestilence or sword" (Ex 5.3). He later gave them other commands in the wilderness, to enhance their relationship to him and to improve the quality of their lives: "Then the Lord commanded us to observe all these statutes, to fear the Lord our God, for our lasting good, so as to keep us alive" (Dt 6.24).

The Almighty does not rush things. He did not bring the Israelites swiftly to their destined goal. They were forty years in the desert or wilderness, before reaching the Promised Land. During that lengthy period, he tested them, to learn how sincere and genuine they were, and to make them ready for their new abode – "testing you to know what was in your heart, whether or not you would keep his commandments" (Dt 8.2). He for his part was always good to them and could challenge them to recognize this: "These forty years the Lord your God has been with you; you have lacked nothing" (Dt 2.7). Even though he may have seemed distant, he was constantly with them, in their long period of transition.

Spiritual Meaning

The liberation of his people from slavery in Egypt has often been regarded by spiritual writers as portraying what is involved in God's freeing all from the prison of sin. This imagery is frequently used by them about carnal evil, and how the Creator helps to liberate those caught in its tyranny.

The Israelites by themselves were unable to bring about their own freedom. They needed leadership and assistance for this. They first had to be given a divinely appointed leader, to direct them towards a new venture. But they required more – God's mighty hand – to be with them, as they wrenched themselves from the dominion of the Egyptians. Sinners, too, have to be inspired by a leader of some kind (perhaps by a preacher), but they also have to get special strength from outside, in order to take steps to change their situation. They need too to taste, in some sense, in advance the delight that conversion brings, and feel a desire to begin a reformed existence.

All religious growth can be viewed as a movement from the slavery of sin or from spiritual inadequacy to the light and freedom of God's kingdom. It has to be a part of an individual's whole life. It therefore involves a long spiritual journey across difficult terrain, where problems, trials and temptations are encountered, before hopefully reaching a final repose of peace and joy. At times, blind faith and trust in the Almighty alone can keep the traveller heading in the right direction, amidst the dominant preoccupations and complexities of life and the dreariness and frustrations of a long march. During this course, it is easy to become impatient, to stumble and then lose heart. It can seem more attractive, when the pace is tough, to ignore God and his commands – especially when the benefits of being faithful to him are not immediately felt as satisfying. What is straightaway gratifying appeals very strongly, when the pressures and tensions of life are acute.

Difficult To Be Faithful

When Moses revealed all the commands that God had made known to him in the wilderness, the people rather enthusiastically, but overconfidently, promised that they would obey: "All the words that the Lord has spoken we will do" (Ex 24.3). Such a spontaneous response is easier given than kept. All turn too readily aside from the Lord's ways! This happened in the case of the Israelites, and the Bible indicates why it was so. They forgot God's words and counsel; they gave too much importance to food and drink; they did not bear in mind the marvels that the Almighty had previously done for them. They lost hope in the promised land – it seemed too far away in the distance. They mingled with the people of other nations and followed their practices (cf Ps 106). Briefly, they were no longer sufficiently focussed on God and they got lost in other more immediate concerns.

Wickedness gains a strong foothold, when the awareness of the Almighty and the need to serve him are not as sharply experienced as they should be. Evil, perceived in advance with its glistening promises, can be most enticing. "For the fascination of wickedness obscures what is good, and roving desire perverts the innocent mind" (Wis 4.12). A spiritual outlook may fade away, when challenged by the apparent brilliance of sin. And as a result, wild desires become very unruly.

Obedience to the Creator fosters the surest way of life, one like his – a holy one. "You shall be holy, for I the Lord your God am holy" (Lev 19.2). This involves having many qualities, faith, control, wisdom, uprightness and personal unity.

The Healing Aspect Of Divine Love

The Israelites' failure to respond to God's directives brought to light not only the divine anger, but more so another more dominant quality of his love, namely his readiness to forgive. Scripture leaves no doubt about God's serious and negative response to evil and warns: "Do not delay to turn back to the Lord ... for suddenly his wrath will come upon you" (cf Sir 5.6-7). His anger, in relation to us, is temporary and at the service of love. Far more important and enduring is another characteristic of his, his pardoning love. "The Lord, the Lord, a God merciful and gracious, slow to anger, and abounding in steadfast love and faithfulness ... yet by no means clearing the guilty" (Ex 34.6,7). The sinner does not escape unscathed, but is still within the wide embrace of love. A main aim of the Almighty is to correct and purify those who err. He searches out to find the wayward, and treats them with his healing and saving power.

7

Further Manifestations Of God's Love In The Old Testament

The history of Israel brought to light many other aspects of God's love, as he formed, strengthened, rebuked, scattered and in part restored his people. A basic law was laid down for them – that it was necessary to be faithful to the Creator, in order to prosper and be secure: "Hear therefore, O Israel, observe them (the commandments) diligently, so that it may go well with you" (Deut 6.13). The primary loyalty needs to be given to him: "The Lord, your God, you shall fear; him you shall serve" (Deut 6.13). A failure to do this would bring about dire consequences: "If you do forget the Lord your God and follow other gods to serve and worship them, I solemnly warn you today that you shall surely perish" (Deut 8.19). Idolatry is clearly a grave sin – and it may be more common than is realized! It was or is not the case that the Almighty is vindictive, but that things are so arranged and linked together, that serious errors somehow bring or drive individuals against unfavourable currents or into unattractive channels, where life becomes hard for them, and they have to struggle more than if they had not sinned!

By choosing David and his successor Solomon to be leaders of a powerful kingdom, God gave a foretaste of Someone more royal who was to follow, and of a more important and better regime (cf 2 Sam 7.13). It would be a divine one – the Lord's very own (cf Lk 1.33), which was described in this way: "Your kingdom is an everlasting kingdom, and your dominion endures throughout all generations" (Ps 145.13). No indication was given as to when this would come about. In the turmoil that followed Solomon's death, the one political territory was split, with two kingdoms emerging, Judah and Israel. The previously strong establishment lost its cohesion and spirit, and selfishness and greed became rampant. Both Israel and Judah in the main neglected God, and the rich significantly behaved unjustly. Yet there were some who tried to correct the situation by their preaching – an important few.

The Prophets

Their main teaching can be summed up as a call to appreciate and to respect God profoundly – to listen to him, and to avoid displeasing him, particularly in key ways. Their frequent plea is: "Hear the word of the Lord" (Hos 4.1). Loving always means paying attention to the ideas of the loved one. In the case of the Almighty this is enormously significant. Those who listen to him are elevated, since they receive an uplifting message from on high, which ennobles them.

Even the prophets themselves, as for example Ezekiel, had to give ear carefully to the divine words: "All my words that I shall speak to you receive in your heart and hear with your ears" (Ez 3.10). It is interesting that listening with the heart is mentioned first – being the most important! It means accepting what God says with love. He himself was asked to eat a scroll, that is to absorb it thoroughly (3.1-3). What a preacher proclaims ought to be first living and vibrant in himself.

Hosea laments that the people haven't a proper relationship with God. When the vertical dimension is faulty, evils on the horizontal plane follow. "Hear the word of the Lord, O people of Israel. … There is no faithfulness or loyalty, and no knowledge of God in the land. Swearing, lying and murder, and stealing and adultery break out" (Hos 4.1-2). Lack of respect for the Creator, which is a form of behaving falsely, begins the downward trend. Without faith in him, the spiritual backbone which supports good conduct is broken, and without it individuals easily lose proper balance! A strong pull to the Creator requires correspondingly good conduct in other areas, and, in fact, motivates it, though individuals may also have to be reminded of their horizontal obligations! The prophets were vividly aware of what came first and so kept repeating the call to return to God.

Within this fundamental vision, they stressed the need for justice – justice in or with faith. "Hear this you who trample upon the needy, and bring the power of the land to an end" (Amos 8.4). "The corruption of Ephraim is revealed, and the wicked deeds of Samaria, for they deal falsely; the thief breaks in and the bandits raid without" (Hos 7.1). "They (the wicked) have grown fat and sleek. They know no bounds in deeds of wickedness; they judge not with justice the cause of the fatherless, to make it prosper, and they do not defend the rights of the needy" (Jer 5. 28). To be correct in one's dealings and to have a genuine concern for the poor are demanded, in order to show true respect to the Lord.

These seers or preachers reminded all to trust in the Creator, but not to have a reckless confidence in him. His might is evident in these following ways. At times, he is ready to rescue the Israelites: "Do not be afraid of the king of Babylon, as you have been; do not be afraid of him, says the

Lord, for I am with you, to save you and to rescue you from his hand" (Jer 42.11). But the reality can be entirely different: "Besiegers come from a distant land; … Your ways and your doings have brought this upon you. This is your doom; and it is bitter. It has reached your very heart" (Jer 4.16,18). Life's happenings and historical events are used by the Almighty for his own purpose. His hand can be active in them in various manners – so it is important to read a situation correctly. In doing this, a fundamental fact has to be kept in mind: the Creator does not let the wicked off with their wrongdoing: "The Lord will by no means clear the guilty" (Nah 1.3). There is always a price to be paid for wickedness! "Therefore thus says the Lord of hosts: 'I will now refine and test them, for what else can I do with my sinful people'?" (Jer 9.7). Yet repentance can weaken his resolve. "But if that nation, concerning whom I have spoken, turns from its evil, I will change my mind about the disaster that I intended to bring on it" (Jer 18.8).

The Lord shows great mastery and love in dealing with the sinner. His anger is always part of his mercy, and however extreme it may seem, it still has a loving side. "In overflowing wrath for a moment I hid my face from you, but with everlasting love I will have compassion on you" (Is 54.8). "His anger lasts but a moment" (Ps 30.5).

In general, the prophets were concerned that their listeners show due respect to the Creator and give heed to what he desires. He should be the brightness that illumines all their living, and, as is stressed by these seers, their dealings with others.

Wisdom

Wisdom is a divine guiding light or instruction from on high. "For the Lord gives wisdom, from his mouth come knowledge and understanding" (Prov 2.6). It comes from him, who "is just in all his ways, and kind in all his doings" (Ps 145.17). It directs those who accept it along a correct and sure way of life: "When you walk, you will not be hampered; and if you run, you will not stumble" (Prov 4.12). By means of this blessing, the Lord accompanies and protects people, being "a shield for those who walk blamelessly, guarding the paths of justice and preserving the way of his faithfulness" (Prov 2.7,8). While it is a gift from above, it can be sought for. The psalmist eagerly prays for this, when he pleads: "Make me to know your ways, O Lord; teach me your paths. Lead me in your truth, and teach me, for you are the God of my salvation" (Ps 25.4). This anticipates the three roles that Christ plays in each life – as the way, the truth and the life (Jn 14.6). As the sapiential literature of the Bible so emphatically stresses, it should be searched for as a priority, since it protects and uplifts (Both "it" and "she" are used for wisdom here): "Get wisdom; get insight.

... Do not forsake her, and she will keep you; love her and she will safeguard you. The beginning of wisdom is this: Get wisdom, and whatever else you get, get insight. Prize her highly, and she will exalt you" (Wis 4.5-8). The nobility she offers is marvellous. She makes people confident too (Prov 3.26).

Wisdom, personified, is recognized as being very close to the Almighty: "She glorifies her noble birth by living with God, and the Lord of all loves her" (Wis 8.3). She knows the divine mind and is a co-worker with him. "She is an initiate in the knowledge of God and an associate in his work" (Wis 8.4). She understands his depths. She conveys such wonderful knowledge to others and inspires love for the Creator in them. The bride, in the Song Of Songs, filled with love, appeals for a continual gift of divine wisdom: "O that you would kiss me with the kisses of your mouth" (1.2). This is interpreted as meaning, "O that you would embrace me with your wisdom" (Origen). It is possible to fall spiritually in love with her: "I desired to take her for my bride, and became enamoured of her beauty" (Wis 8.2). This desire marks a rich state of soul.

Wisdom has enormous gifts to bestow: "I have good advice and sound wisdom; I have insight, I have strength. ... Riches and honour are with me, enduring wealth and prosperity" (Prov 8.14,18). Yet when these blessings are absent, individuals may wonder if she has deserted them. Yet allowance has to be made for the mysteriousness of divine wisdom. Her riches may be hiddenly there, in very adverse situations!

The advice it offers at a given time may seem beyond the capability of the ordinary person to fulfil, such as: "Delay not to give to the needy" (Sir 4.3). Yet it must be remembered that wisdom always calls for greatness, since it sets before us God's thinking and attitudes, which we find hard to cope with.

It only finds a proper place in the lives of those who live uprightly – it does not dwell in the sinner (Wis 1.4). Living in a manner pleasing the Creator is a necessary step towards being blessed with this sure favour. "If you desire wisdom, keep the commandments, and the Lord will lavish her upon you" (Sir 1.26).

Prayer Needed

All have to respond to the Creator with and in prayer. He is to be worshipped – adoration being the deepest and most wholehearted answer to him. "O come, let us worship and bow down, / Let us kneel before the Lord, our Maker!" (Ps 95.6). This is best done in his holy temple, or while turned in this direction. "I will worship toward thy holy temple in the fear of thee". (Ps 5.7).

Thanks and praise have to be offered to him. "Give thanks to the Lord of hosts, for the Lord is good, for his steadfast love endures for ever" (Jer 33.11). The Psalms tell us to bear in mind especially one characteristic of his, his loving kindness, when we exalt him. "The Lord is merciful and gracious, slow to anger and abounding in steadfast love" (Ps 103.8). It is most fitting to acknowledge this quality – "to declare your steadfast love in the morning and your faithfulness by night" (Ps 92.1,2). The truth, that the Lord loves us dearly, no matter what our circumstances, is a most assuring comfort. "Great is his steadfast love towards us" (Ps 117.2).

Because the Lord is of such a kind, he is most approachable, even particularly so, when we are in greatest need. He is open to human appeals, and so the psalmist can confidently pray: "Give ear to my words, O Lord; give heed to my sighing. Listen to the sound of my cry" (Ps 5.1,2,7). It is marvellous that the Lord listens to our feeble cries and even distressful shrieks. "He is near to all who call upon him" (Ps 145.18). Those who adequately respect him receive many benefits as a result: "He fulfils the desire of all who fear him, he also hears their cry and saves them" (Ps 145.19). He aids the struggling and faltering: "The Lord upholds all who are falling, and raises up all who are bowed down" (Ps 145. 14).

The sinner asks pardon for his transgressions, knowing how merciful the Lord is. "Be mindful of your mercy, O Lord, and of your steadfast love, for they have been from of old. Do not remember the sins of my youth, nor my transgressions" (Ps 25.6,7). The repentant guilty ask God to let his forgiving kindness bear down on them. The wonderful psalm, which begins with these words, "Have mercy on me, O God, according to your steadfast love; according to your abundant mercy blot out my transgressions" (Ps 51.1), is the plea of a sinner, who is very conscious of the wickedness which clings so closely and who seeks a thorough renewal through the creative power of the Almighty. The Lord always pardons and cures – forgiving all iniquity and healing all diseases (Ps 103.3). No matter how wicked sinners may be, they should know that, if they seek help, the Lord's steadfast love and plenteous redemption will not be wanting. A willingness to pardon always shows the greatness of love.

Images Describing God's Love

The close relationship between God and his people (and so of each one) is more intimate than that between a mother and a child: "Can a woman forget her suckling child, or show no compassion for the child of her womb? Even these may forget, yet I will not forget you" (Is 49.15). The Creator is a father, who acts with the tenderness of a mother. "As a mother comforts her child, so will I comfort you" (Is 66.13). "As a father has compassion for his children, so the Lord pities those who fear him" (Ps 103.13). It is, however, only as a Father that he is revealed: "If then I am a Father, where is the honour due to me?" (Mal 1.6). "Do you thus repay the Lord, O foolish and senseless people? Is not he your father, who created you, who made you and established you?" (Deut 32.6).

Another important image to describe the partnership between God and his people is that of a groom and bride, as in the *Song Of Songs*. The marvellous commentaries on this book, by Origen, Gregory of Nyssa and others, highlight the splendour and mystery of divine love, the yearnings of the creature for the presence of the loved One, and the beauty, attraction and joy that radiate from the divine Spouse to the pure bride. Alas, the harmony between the two lovers is not always as smooth nor as sublime as it should be. God is also presented in the Bible as a married man, who struggles with an unfaithful wife (Jer 2; Hos 1-2; 3.1-5). The human response to the Beloved is not always as wholehearted or as transparent as it should be, and may be very faltering, even in a serious way. Still the groom keeps beckoning to go to him, the flawless One.

The Lord is also called a pastor who tends his flock – an image that is prominent in the NT. "The Lord is my shepherd, I shall not want" (Ps 23.1). But the sheep are hard to control, being like a stubborn heifer (Hos 4.16). Yet the supreme pastor does not easily give up. He is also looked on as a healer (Jer 3.22), a saviour (Is 43.3) and a redeemer (Is 44.6).

Note

The OT, as well as the NT, needs to be read and cherished as an expression of the greatness, depth, goodness and immensity of God's love. The more each person becomes acquainted with the text, and senses its wonder and vitality, the more the divine world is opened up, in its splendour, wonder and richness.

8

God As Love Revealed in Christ

The NT makes plain that God and his love are identical: "God is love" (1 Jn 4.8). And fittingly enough, the most appropriate way to establish a relationship with him is through love – not through reasoning! "The one who does not love does not know God" (Ibid).

The Creator deals always with us in a spirit of love, and he demands the same of us: "You shall love the Lord your God with all your heart, and with all your soul, and with all your mind, and with all your strength" (Mk 12.30) – a little more detailed than the same command given in the OT (Deut 6.5). He wants a clear and total response from us in this regard – something very demanding for the volatile and scattered human heart. The second commandment "You shall love your neighbour as yourself" (cf Mk 12.31) is made even more exigent by Jesus: "Just as I have loved you, you also should love one another" (Jn 13.14) – that is giving one's life. These two mighty demands, which seem excessive from a merely human point of view, merge into one and have to be fulfilled together. "Those who love God must love their brothers and sisters also" (1 Jn 4.21). The call of love is to be open to all and to yield to immensity.

Made Known By Jesus

The Almighty's love was mainly manifested, when he sent his Son on earth: "God's love was revealed among us in this way: God sent his only Son into the world, so that we might live through him" (1 Jn 4.9). He came as life-bringing. He wanted to exalt greatly our living – making us deeply like his Son. "For God so loved the world that he gave his only Son, so that everyone who believes in him may not perish but have eternal life" (Jn 3.16). With the Son he gave us all (Rom 8.32). The Creator put himself out enormously in the person of Jesus to redeem us from sin and to sanctify us. He lowered himself to such an extent, so as to be able to face humanity at its meanest and wickedest. By dying on the cross and rising from the dead, he scattered his spiritual power, which touches every life with divine brilliance and goodness.

In this most generous gesture of the Son's surrendering and taking up his life, love at its unsurpassable marvel is found. Because of this, we need to bow often in reverence before Christ, bearing in mind his excellent and mysterious kindness, while being thankful to him. It is no wonder that John stresses that God loved us first, and that our attempts at doing the same are only responses to his initiative (1 Jn 4.10). The inspiration or invitation to do so and the pull to it proceed from him, before we comply in any way. We easily underestimate the force of his redeeming love in our lives!

When we come to consider Jesus Christ, we are faced with his immensity. We can approach him under many titles, such as Saviour, Christ, Lord, the resurrected One, the Bringer of peace, our Helper and Protector. No matter which one of these we focus on, we still only recognize part of him. We have an impressive vision of him, when we regard him as "our wisdom, our righteousness and sanctification and redemption" (1 Cor 1.30), but it all is in relation to ourselves. The fullest title we can give him is that he is the Son of God – as in the first line in Mark's Gospel: "The beginning of the gospel of Jesus Christ, the Son of God" (1.1).

Even though Jesus is treated here under very important aspects, they by no means exhaust all that could be said about him.

Love As Salvific

Jesus came on earth with a definite purpose – to bring salvation to all. This was stressed at his birth: "This day is born to you in Bethlehem a Saviour, who is Christ the Lord" (Lk 2.11). His message is presented as one of salvation: "Repent and believe in the message of salvation" (Mk 1.15). Redemption is the word used for his salvific work. This has two aspects: "God sent his Son to be the atoning sacrifice for our sins" (1 Jn 4.10). The other dimension is: "I have come that they may have life and have it abundantly" (Jn 10.10). The Son changes the thrust of people's lives. "And he died for all, that those who live might live no longer for themselves, but for him who for their sake died and was raised" (2 Cor 5.15). This is brought about through faith and regeneration: "He who believes and is baptized will be saved" (Mk 16.16). It calls for listening to his words, which are spirit and life (Jn 6.63).

Salvation is realized partly on earth, but mainly in heaven. The believer down below has a foothold in the next life – being like a house built on solid rock (Mt 7.24ff) (so indestructible!). The one with faith is mainly orientated upwards, to the salvation that is realized on high – following Jesus' advice: "Do not store up for yourselves treasures on earth, where moth and rust destroy, but lay up treasures in heaven" (Mk 6.19). The

Lord's instruction about entering through the narrow gate (Lk 13.24) and being ready for the master's return (Lk 12.36) calls for choosing wisely and keeping the final end in mind.

The Son's activity down below aimed at bringing sanctity and wholeness to those who accepted him. He was revealing and living out "the goodness and loving kindness of God our Saviour" (Tit 3.4). He wanted all to lead fruitful lives. What he desired, and still does, is very different from a successful, worldly life: "For whoever would save his life would lose it; and whoever loses his life for my sake and the gospel's will save it" (Mk 8.36).

Christ's miracles, mainly restoring people to good health, manifest his deep concern to relieve human suffering, and are a prelude to a more complete revitalization and transformation afterwards. Salvation has an earthly dimension, involving liberation from everything that oppresses people. Many are gravely distressed or hampered in life – imprisoned, in pain, poor or oppressed. The Son's work is set to remedy all such ailments – though in stages. The wonders he accomplished highlight what for the most part is being achieved in an assured, though less sensational, long-term manner. His miracles serve mainly to draw attention to his message, and the profound, religious change that this achieves. The healing of a blind man (Mk 8.22-26) and a deaf one (Mk 7.31-37) have to be placed in the wider context of Jesus inviting all to open their spiritual eyes and ears, in order to see and hear more: "Come and see" (Jn 1.46); "Whoever has ears to hear ought to hear" (Lk 10.24). Jesus' feeding the hungry with miraculous bread (Mk 6.34-44) is a foretaste of his creating heavenly food out of his own flesh – the gift that especially brings salvation: "Whoever eats my flesh and drinks my blood has eternal life, and I will raise him up on the last day" (Jn 6.54).

He himself is not just the bringer of salvation, but embodies it. When he visits Zacchaeus, he can say "today salvation has come to this house" (Lk 19.9). Briefly, Christ himself is our salvation. "And this is eternal life, that they may know thee the only true God, and Jesus Christ whom thou hast sent" (Jn 17).

The Way, The Truth, And The Life

Jesus is all three (Jn 14.6). These are aspects of his life, which emphasize his salvific love. We can view them in another manner, in line with his three roles, as priest (life-giving), prophet (teaching), king (directing). It may not be going too far to regard them as follows; the way, as what is good, the truth, and the life, as what is beautiful. Anyway, a consideration of them shows the extent and depth which Christ's presence can have in each life.

The Way

He is the way, not only because he opens up a secure path forward for all, but because he himself is that very thing – an ever expanding course. All genuine spiritual progress is an advance in him! By staying close to and by being mysteriously united with him, opportunities open out for us, even where otherwise there seems to be little prospect. When the future looks uncertain, and things appear very much on the decline, remaining with Christ is the surest position to adopt. Sooner or later, accessible stretches forward are made available and offered to us!

All Christ's life is movement, into which we are drawn. Even in the Blessed Trinity he receives his very self from the Father and returns that to him – continuously getting and giving back. While on earth he came from above and was always in the process of returning to the One who sent him. While dwelling among us, he was unhesitatingly committed to what was expected of him, ever obeying the One who sent him. He never deviated into a wrong path. He finds a place for us all in his mysterious journey to the Father.

His is the living reality of all that is said about the way in the OT. He embraces in himself the directives given there about the path to follow. The very recognition of the Lord ensures safe and guided travel forwards. "In all your ways acknowledge him(the Lord), and he will make straight your paths" (Prov 3.6). God leads people by a direct path, though they may feel that their journey is not so straight. Even though "some (Israelites) wandered in desert wastes, finding no way to a city to dwell in … he led them by a straight path" (Ps 107.4,7). What appeared to them as roundabout travel was in God's eyes a direct route. It should have brought them happiness! "Happy are those who keep my ways" (Prov 8.32).

When the psalmist sees danger lurking near him, he rightly prays to the Lord: "In the path where I walk they have hidden a trap for me. I look to the right and watch, but there is no one who takes notice of me. … I cry to thee, O Lord" (Ps 142. 3-5). He protects those in danger, who trust in him: "Even though I walk through the valley of the shadow of death, I fear no evil; for thou art with me" (Ps 23.4).

Walking correctly means being in step with Jesus. All the Son's activities on earth were manifestations of him as the way – whether walking by the sea of Galilee or up to Jerusalem. They are the paths along which he in part accomplished his redemptive work. Lingering with him along these tracts is always very spiritually enriching. We haven't walked sufficiently in mind and heart with him. But it is above all his passion and death which show most intensively the path he has chosen. We may fear greatly this portion or stage of his life. Yet pondering over his sufferings amounts to travelling profoundly with him, on his path of extreme charity. Even more so is dying and rising with him.

Jesus summed up what is called for very briefly, in the words, "Follow me" or "Come after me". His true followers keep their eyes fixed on him, and are guided by him. "The sheep hear his voice, and he calls his own sheep by name and leads them out" (Jn 10.3). Wherever he goes, he must be followed. An important kind of travel demanded of some is to respond to his missionary call. "Go out into the whole world and preach the gospel to the whole creation" (Mk 16.15). His way is very varied and extends far, but is always an upright and wise one.

The Truth

The road which the Son of God stands for – and which he himself is – is the truest or wisest one possible. The knowledge that Christ gives opens out further and extends the path forward. "The ways of the Lord are truth" (Ps 25.10). They are divinely illuminated. "I am the light of the world. Whoever follows me will not walk in darkness" (Jn 8.12). Whoever ignores or moves away from him is left in confusion and blindness: "Whoever walks in the dark does not know where they are going" (Jn 12.35). The direction to be taken often has to be chosen, and must be embarked on, aided by divine wisdom.

Jesus is the truth, because he reveals the Father, and "the manifold wisdom of God" (Eph 3.10). The true path forward has to lie in his truth. Christ asks for this for his disciples, before he departs: "Sanctify them in the truth; thy word is truth " (Jn 17.17). He himself is God's wisdom (1 Cor 1.24; Jn 1.1), a living person, created at the beginning of all (Prov 8.28). He in his incarnation is the exposition of the Father to the world. "I revealed your name (the Father's truth) to those whom you gave me out of the world" (Jn 17.6) – something that the Son alone is aware of (Mt 11.27). He makes known the greatness of the Creator and his full involvement in the world, conveying this most important knowledge. He has a clear mandate: "I say only what the Father taught me" (Jn 8.28). To follow him is to live in his word. It means to spiritually travel along a sure, bright and enlightened path, ever deepening into the mystery of God's truth. The psalmist, while not openly knowing Christ, prays for this: "Teach me thy way, O Lord, that I may walk in thy truth" (Ps 86.11). The follower of Jesus asks for divine wisdom, to know better the thinking of God.

The truth that Jesus offers, and which he himself is, is the revealing of God's creative thought in a manner that we can perceive. This shows up our own limited grasp of things and the confined way in which we see them. It, to take one example, pulls us towards what we might not like to do, as in the command "Love your enemies" (Lk 6.27). Paul knows how precious and how powerful such knowledge is, when he prays for the Ephesians, that "the father of glory give you a spirit of wisdom and revelation to know him" (Eph 1.17). To acquire such a vision, the eyes of the heart have to be enlightened first (Eph 1.18).

Truth and light are one in God. The psalmist regards God's commands as a form of light. "Thy word is a lamp to my feet, and a light to my path" (Ps 119. 105). Listening to the Almighty means receiving his clarity: "The unfolding of thy words gives light" (Ps 119. 30). The biblical expression "to walk in the law of the Lord" means to live in his truth. Paul has no doubt but that we should choose such a path: "Walk as children of light" (Eph 5.8). Jesus as the truth deepens, enriches and brightens his way for us.

The path of truth along which Christ leads us may not be at times as joyful as we would like it to be. If our path entails carrying the cross, there may well be for us desolation within – and darkness over the earth. When this is so, we have to find light and meaning for our situation, while praying before Jesus on the cross. His suffering there can assuage and give some sense to any painful and obscure experience of ours. By staying with him in his pain, we gain strength and consolation which enable us to endure our own difficulties.

The Life

He also is the life, giving his divine vitality to all who receive him. Going his way is not only entering into his truth, but sharing in his existence. Jesus is life in a wholly special sense, since he is God. His living stretches both before and beyond his time on earth, and moves in the sphere of the divine. It is an unending life, most full and infinitely whole. It is one that is united with the Father through the power of the Holy Spirit. Sharing in that life amounts to entering into the mystery of God in a living way. "All things were made through him" (Jn 1.3).

St Paul sees all genuine growth or advancement as a construction in him: "As therefore you received Christ Jesus the Lord, so live in him, rooted and built up in him and established in the faith" (Col 2.6). To be alive in its deepest sense is to be in him. This is why he came on earth: "I have come, so that they may have life and have it more abundantly" (Jn 10.10). What is at stake is his own resurrected life, which he shares with others. It is the most exalted living possible for us, and due to the Almighty's generosity. It is begun down here below: "For just as the Father raises the dead and gives life, so also does the Son give life to whoever he wishes" (Jn 5.21).

Moving along his truthful path has a deeper aspect – that of "being in him". The result is a new creation. "Abide in me as I abide in you. I am the vine, you are the branches. He who abides in me , and I in him, he it is that bears much fruit, for apart from me you can do nothing" (Jn 15.4,5). The power or spiritual energy which surges from there leads to much achieving: "Those who abide in me and I in them bear much fruit" (Jn 15.5). Such genuine accomplishing is eternal and abides forever. Whenever something lasting is being brought about, the deepest influential factor at work there is the love between the Father and the Son, spreading outwards and bearing down on a particular incident. The Father's love initiates all. "As the Father has loved me, so I have loved you. Remain in my love" (Jn 15.9). Divine life and love are the same.

Christ's life in all its aspects indicates love. All his dealings and actions, every gesture and journey of his, his praying and sleeping are expressions of that same. Sharing in his existence calls for lingering with him in his earthly scenes. The believer should be consciously with him, as much as possible, receiving more and more vitality from him. Such spiritual energy is enormous, and gives inestimable beauty and value to each.

*   *   *   *

John several times focuses on the Christian life, with these aspects in mind. "If you abide in me (life), and my words (the truth) abide in you, ask for whatever you wish, and it will be done for you (finding the way) (Jn 15.7). The whole process is again described in this manner: "Those who love me (choose his way) keep my word (the truth), and my Father will love them, and we will come to them and make our home with them (a community of life)" (Jn 14.23). Jesus the way opens up the path forward, illumines it with his creative light or wisdom, and gives life, which ever leads to deeper communion in love with him.

Acquiring salvation, however complicated it may appear, is a unity, in its movement, inspired insight or vision and divine satisfaction. It is following the Son, the way, the truth and the life. His whole life on earth, his words and actions, all tending towards the cross and resurrection, have to be considered as bringing salvation.

9

The Cross – The Supreme Manifestation Of Love

The very mention of the word "cross" immediately evokes a sense of horror and disgust within us. If we give much thought to it, we tend to become saddened by this dismal side of life. It shows up human cruelty at its worst – bringing about the death of a fellow person in the most painful and savage manner possible. Even if we think that an individual enduring such or a similar fate was wicked and deserved some correction and curtailment, we know that the very option for capital punishment, however mildly administered, goes too far and is utterly lacking in charity – depriving a person of the chance to repent. That the Son of God had to die in this most painful way may strike us as outrageous, and we may wonder how could it have happened. There is nothing in its outlandishness and barbarity, looked at in itself and from the side of those who carry it out, which makes us think of love. From our side, it seems only vicious and heartless. Even the generosity and nobility of a patriot who has been executed tend to be obscured by the brutality involved! It is a topic that is almost unsuitable for our thinking. A happening of this kind belongs to the darkest side of human existence. It makes us too conscious of "man's inhumanity to man". How wicked we are capable of being!

Jesus' Terrible Death

In view of what has been said above, we may be very casual about the Son of God's death, and have inadequate interest in it. We know that, while its hour lasted, it was horrendous, but now feel relieved that it is over. We may gloss over his wounds and pain with a happier vision, dwelling on his serenity, generosity and love, and forget their raw and grim aspect! We readily cast the blame on his contemporaries for not understanding him better, and for rejecting him so drastically. Though we are intellectually aware that all of us, on account of our sins, are responsible for his sufferings, we don't normally allow that fact to cause us much emotional discomfort! After all, others are as guilty as we are. We feel too that we can eliminate greatly the need to reflect on his pain by simply giving thanks to him! We also find comfort – to our relief – in the truth that Christ chose this way to redeem and save us. And we may even entertain the view that there is some liking in God for what is harsh, painful and difficult! It is puzzling why he made such a choice – to send his Son to suffer and to die for us – when there may have been easier possibilities open for him!

Still we have to incline towards the opinion that this may well be the manner which best expresses God's super-abundant love, and that it was the most loving way to redeem us – as Dante pointed out. God's choice and action bring together many different and mysterious elements, his absolute love, his total rejection of sin, his mercy on the sinner, and his desire to train and involve all in the process of freeing themselves from sin. The path he took manifests mercy at its best and sin at its wickedest. It involves the supremest triumph through the greatest failure. If Jesus had to suffer so much to redeem and save us, the malice of evil must be very great! We only realize its gravity, when, with a generous heart, we sense the horror of the cross and the extremeness of Christ's sufferings. Because he was willing to endure so much, his love for us must be enormous! It is on Calvary too that we best discover the depths of true love, and how self-sacrificing it is.

Jesus had to pay dearly for our sins. Such wickedness was challenged, faced up to, and destroyed by him. The full fury of evil and the force of its devastating aggressiveness assailed him, bringing about his cruel end. Sin there showed its total malice – for what worse can it do? It is argued, with strong claims, that the Father expressed his horror of sin, by abandoning Jesus on the cross, as he carried the sin of the world and became identified with it. It is an idea that has to be treated with caution! Could the Son ever have become fully identified with evil? While this latter went very far or touched its lowest depths, it over-reached itself. For a brief time, it took control over Christ's physical movements, killing him in his humanity. But soon afterwards it lost its grip on him, and had to utterly give way to his divine strength and glory. In reality, in his death Jesus was always in control. He moved along his self-sacrificing way, amid scorn and rejection, in a very self-possessed manner, and, there, was being transformed through his willing acceptance of pain.

His submission to such torture and shame brought to light the tragic side of his wonderful love – a necessary deep element in all true affection or friendship! The tragedy of Christ's death consists in the fact that the one who is absolutely good and great was destroyed, if only for a time, by the folly and smallness of people (all of us). We can do enormous damage, which we are unable to rectify. Yet we can view Christ's horrific end in a different light, since the strings of divine mercy and love are exercised or played out in it. The most sublime grandeur, divine glory with all its achieving power, is present in the emaciated Christ. Even in that condition, the suffering Son of God merits special attention. Though enduring under a terrible strain, he was ever within the embrace of divine love. His darkness was light, a strange paradox. We may wonder how much did he cry at this hour! His was a revolting, yet majestic, departure.

The Son's cruel death reveals the two attitudes of the Creator towards evil – his infinite horror of it and his great regard for the sinner. His intolerance of it is called his anger. Sin has a negative effect on him, causing revulsion and making evident an obscure, unfathomable turbulent side in him! Jesus' death on the cross reveals the troubled darkness of God. No wonder, then, that at such an hour "there was darkness over the earth", since it shared for a time in the divine mysterious obscurity.

The cross is the great school of repentance – if we allow its force and mystery to strike us.

Death As Generous Love

Jesus views his own death in terms of the utmost love: "Greater love has no man than this, that a man lay down his life for his friends" (Jn 15.13). He did not spare himself, but gave himself completely, in order to remedy our greatest burden and problem. "He himself bore our sins in his body upon the cross, so that, free from sins, we might live for righteousness; by his wounds you have been healed" (1 Pet 2.24). The pain that Christ endured provides the total solution for all our ills. We were saved from the futile ways of wickedness by someone very precious – "not with perishable things like silver or gold, but with the precious blood of Christ, like that of a lamb without defect or blemish" (1 Pet 1,18,19).

The result is something extraordinary for many, if not for all – transformation and adornment in an exalted state. "But God, who is rich in mercy, out of the great love with which he loved us, even when we were dead through our transgressions, made us alive together with Christ (by grace you have been saved), and raised us up with him and seated us with him in the heavenly places in Christ Jesus" (Eph 2.4-6). With him, we have begun now our heavenly life – yet only its initial stages. We still await our final redemption (cf Eph 1.18). He is the source, from which that comes (Heb 5.8). He opened up a new path for us, along which we receive instruction and are made long for what is to come. "For the grace of God has appeared, saving all and training us to reject godless ways … as we await the blessed hope, the appearance of the glory of the great God … who gave himself for us" (Tit 2.11-14). The Son endured his terrible ordeal, so that we could live in a selfless manner – turned outwards mainly towards him. "And he died for all, so that those who live might live no longer for themselves, but for him who died and was raised for them" (1 Cor 5.15). He wanted us to be brightly established in him. "For our sake he made him to be sin who did not know sin, so that we might become the righteousness of God in him" (2 Cor 5.21).

It is important for all of us to deeply appreciate the kindness and goodness of God, manifested in his sending his Son on earth, to die for our sins. His sufferings ever teach us how wonderful divine love is.

Thinking On His Death

To appreciate adequately the crucifixion, it has to be dwelt on reverently, that is in a prayerful manner. The inner senses have to become spiritually tender, in order to be moved by the immense goodness and love expressed there. There is no substitute for humbly and quietly meditating on Christ's passion, nor is there any short way of doing this. Not to do so is to remain partially untouched by the peak of his nobility. He can have a powerful influence on us, through his pain on Calvary. The pull to goodness from there is immense.

We may linger with Jesus on the cross occasionally – for a short while during Holy Week, or if some unusual inspiration strikes us or we need to appeal greatly to him. But generally we find it too sad and almost negative to ponder at length over this grim happening. When Christ's love is reduced to pain, we feel very uncomfortable with it. We prefer to picture the Son of God in the more attractive settings of his earthly life, when his power, vigour and warmth are more evident. He appeals especially to us in the idyllic scenes of Galilee. As a result, we really don't travel sufficiently with him in mind and spirit along the way of the cross, and we leave him too alone and abandoned there. We need to stay longer with him! As well, we have to recognize his underlying grandeur and kingly dignity, even in such misery.

We should accompany him in his agony, not just as spectators, but trying to feel inwardly the way he did. In the Garden of Gethsemane, his real fear of the ordeal that lay ahead of him was overcome by his inner strength and fidelity, but for a time he had to keep mastering his feelings, which were urging him to deviate. He set himself fully in one direction – to return to his Father – and was willing to face all, in order to arrive there. "For the joy that was set before him, he endured the cross" (Heb 12.2). The firmness of his resolve to face up to what was laid out for him, on the way of obedience, was unshakeable. That, however did not lessen its severity. Its horror had to be endured moment by moment, in patient loneliness. His disciples failed to stay awake and to be with him – offering no support nor consolation. Perhaps they couldn't, since they weren't able for it – something Jesus may have understood. They reneged on him, while he was being tortured, and they were too stunned and shocked to try anything that might help! Jesus knew that this was the way chosen for him by the Father, and he never had any doubt about its correctness. He was drawing value and blessings out of it for others, while they were solely concerned about themselves.

His arrest and trial allow us to contrast the humility, uprightness and patience of the Son of God with the arrogance, falseness, and vicious impulsiveness of those who caused his death. His behaviour all through his passion differs enormously from the cowardliness and weakness of the others involved in it, and the casual way in which they tolerated or committed evil. Alas, we all are numbered among these latter. Because the authorities neither wanted nor understood him and felt threatened by him, they immediately rejected him and were determined to liquidate him. They preferred their own thinking to that of God, and felt too sure of themselves. They were blinded by the darkness of their anger and became very vicious. They were insensitive to God's wisdom.

Pilate was out of sympathy with the desires of the mob, but he hesitated and fumbled too much. He feared to go against their wishes and reluctantly glided into appeasing them. He failed to take a stand in accordance with what he himself felt. He weakly dissolved into the current of their wickedness, which was rapidly moving against Jesus. Pilate allowed himself to be dragged into that swiftly flowing stream, rather than standing solidly on the bank. He couldn't take an upright position under pressure. He yielded to what for the time being was the easier path, though it was one of darkness. The light was there before him, but it's hidden brightness escaped him. And mysteriously enough it was good for all humanity that it did!

The pain of Jesus grew more extreme, as he was scourged, crowned with thorns and finally crucified – the cruellest method of execution known. He was put to death between two criminals – an indication of the kind of person he was considered to be. One of them was selfishly concerned about himself and any prospects he had, while the other felt respect and reverence for the Son of God. The former's thinking was confined to himself, while the latter was drawn outwards, to Jesus. He even pleaded for the Lord to be kind to him after death. He saw in him a Saviour and a lasting benefactor.

The Son showed the glory of God and his exalted kingliness, as he died. Though in terrible pain on the cross, he displayed his extraordinary inner worth, through his prayer to his Father, his forgiving attitude, hope, and concern for others. He surrendered himself totally to the Father's plan for him. His free and obedient spirit was evident throughout the whole ordeal. He lovingly experienced death in its most complete form. In him now is found the full meaning of every demise. His existence became pain on the cross, though underlying it was far more than that! We can only grope, at best, in our efforts to appreciate the completeness of Calvary.

It is very sobering to seriously recognize that the Son of God had to face the most wretched punishment possible. The response of his own creatures to him was extremely wicked. How could this have happened? Surely God deserved better! Yet if we were alive, when Christ was on earth, would we have reacted any better to him? But the matter is wider and deeper than this. The real cause of his death is the drunkenness or madness which sin brings about in the human heart, and by means of which reality is viewed wrongly, and human behaviour can become aggressively violent. Looking at Jesus' sufferings, we sense the waywardness and vicious daring that result from not being in tune with God – from not listening to Christ and his message. A strong negative reaction to him and his teaching can lead to great criminality. Had his contemporaries fittingly received him, he would not have died! Yet it has to be borne in mind, too, that the Almighty allowed evil to be so powerful and to blind so many, and deliberately exposed his own Son to its force, for his own loving purpose. Jesus was sent to be our Saviour, and the cross was the way chosen for this. Beyond his suffering and death was resurrected life – anticipated strangely enough in the manner in which he endured. The cross reveals a dark and cruel fate, but divine life was shining through it.

It is important for us to see frequently with our inner eyes Christ stretched out on Calvary, while feeling sympathy for him. "The Son of man must be raised up, so that all who believe in him may have eternal life" (Jn 3.14,15). On Calvary, perfect love assailed the sin of the world, and allowed it to be burned in the flame of the human-divine suffering one. Our best approach to this mystery is to consciously and humbly open ourselves in mind and spirit to the dying Christ, in order to be influenced thoroughly by him. We need to admire the Son with tender affection and gaze at him in silence and stupor. We have to ever learn from and enter more deeply into the mystery of God's redeeming love. The lengthier our stay with him, the freer and quicker we will move to a heavenly vision of him – and the shorter will be our detention in purgatory!

Jesus' Suffering And Our Pain

It is his death that gives dignity to all human suffering. His pain underpins all our distresses and sanctifies them. It is a paradox that the cross and glory (suffering and spiritual beauty) go hand in hand. There is real beauty, but also value, in suffering! All that Jesus endured was redemptive, being the fire that consumed wickedness! – and in a mysterious way all ailments are part of this. We should ever look on pain and discomfort in our own lives in a positive light. These may be very trying and wearying, but there is a far brighter side to them.

Resurrection

The cross was followed by Christ's resurrection. He rose from the dead by the power of God. His victory over sin and death became evident, and he could convincingly say: "I died, and behold I am alive for evermore" (Rev 1.17).

Christ, risen from the dead, now sits at the right hand of the Father. There all power is given to him. With the Father, he sends the Spirit of his love or might into the world, to bring his redemptive work fully to an end. He, ascending on high, has opened up the prospect of eternal life for all of us. The better portion has yet to come. This should arouse hope in us, and give us confidence that we are safe and secure, when we follow him.

10

Loving the Neighbour – Especially the Needy

Much emphasis is rightly placed on this nowadays. We are continually reminded by those with a sharp social sense of the acute suffering of the poor and deprived of all sorts – the marginalized and the misfortunate. The media too frequently portray for us the atrociousness of the circumstances of many people's lives, and the vastness of the problem of poverty – which, when we think about it, we find overwhelming. Charity or the law of love demands that we pay attention to and help those in need – ever giving generously.

In the end, the final judgement of each person, according to one approach to it in the NT – the other stresses more belief in Jesus Christ – depends heavily on this: "For I was hungry and you gave me food, I was thirsty and you gave me drink, a stranger and you welcomed me, naked and you clothed me, ill and you cared for me. ... As long as you did it to one of the least of my brothers, you did it to me" (Mt 25.35,40). It is hard to realize that every time some poor person seeks assistance from us, our reaction to such a one will haunt us later, in either a good or a bad way. The measure of generosity demanded of us is enormously great: "Give to everyone who asks you" (Mt 5.42). We may shudder, as we fear that it all is too much for us. We may have to admit that we fail miserably by giving too little. We may offer our well-wishing goodwill, but then shrug our shoulders and wonder what we can do. God alone can always bestow freely, and each of us shares in his Spirit or grace, when we act accordingly. So we are ever challenged to be more at one with the Creator, in his readiness to give.

As Christ

The Son of God showed the wholeheartedness of his active love for his creatures, in both word and deed. "For you know the grace of our Lord Jesus Christ, that though he was rich, yet for your sake he became poor, so that by his poverty you might become rich" (2 Cor 8.9).

The extent to which the Son of God was willing to offer and surrender himself to redeem and save all, from eternal destruction, and grant them eternal life, is enormous and most wonderful. "For though he was in the form of God, he did not regard equality with God something to be clung to, but emptied himself, taking the form of a slave ... he humbled himself, becoming obedient to death, even death on a cross" (Phil 2.6-8). How concerned about us God proved to be! The immensity of his love towards us is best grasped, as has been seen, by seriously reflecting on Christ's terrible death. "But God proves his love for us in that while we were sinners Christ died for us" (Rom 5.8). In our greatest need, Jesus came to our aid. He, however, did more than embody and exemplify the extreme largesse of God. He draws us to share in his actions, bringing us along with him. Everything he did was with open, embracing hands – making it possible for us to take part in it. He instructs us too and helps us to be like him in his self-giving for others. The parable of the good Samaritan outlines a divine path of love which we should follow. We have to allow the vivacity of its teaching to be vibrant in us, in our own daily living.

A Story Of Love – The Good Samaritan

There are various interpretations of this marvellous composition. According to an old one, by Severus of Antioch and Maximus the Confessor, Christ himself is the good Samaritan, who finds humanity wounded and in distress, and responds with love and help. Going down to Jericho amounts to moving towards what is "low-lying and stifled in heat – meaning the ardent life of this world, which separates from God and drags down, which causes suffocation in the heat of shameful desire, and chokes to death". The brigands are a swarm of demons, who strip humanity of its cloak of virtue. The Mosaic law was not adequate for the situation (the priest and levite). The wine poured on the wounds is the Word – instructive but pungent. The inn to which the wounded is brought is the Church. The man in charge there stands for the apostles and their successors. This interpretation has much to commend it. And it would be useful for all of us to regard Christ as the good Samaritan.

However, the more usual way of viewing the happening is still valid and instructive. It brings out most clearly the pressing demands of charity. The story is well-known. A man went down from Jerusalem to Jericho – even still a lonely road, through barren and rocky hills. While he was travelling alone, robbers attacked and robbed him. They wounded him too, to weaken him, so that they could escape, without any alarm being raised. The poor man was left half-dead – gravely wounded and unable to move.

A priest happened to be going along the same route. Chance

occurrences may pressingly claim our attention and make urgent demands on us. He saw the suffering man, but, alas, passed him by. He might have had other important engagements to attend to. There is no indication that he sought anyone else to help out, if he was too busy himself. The sad fact is that he did not stop even briefly, which would indicate some degree of yielding to the situation, but completely ignored the person in a grave condition. He did not draw near to him, but remained distant, and tried to escape from the problem. In brief, he totally failed to respond to another's urgent distress. A person so ill must be given assistance as a priority!

Love draws people close to each other, and should do so especially to the needy and suffering, but selfishness keeps them apart.The priest, alas, kept aloof, remaining closed in his own world and not moving out in either spirit or body to the ailing man. He did not allow the wounded one to impinge deeply on him. He did not really sense the other's feelings. Beyond seeing him, he did not meet him. The Levite who went along the same road behaved no differently. More was expected of him too.

The reaction of the Samaritan was quite remarkable. The fact that the suffering person belonged to another nationality and religion did not matter to him nor deter him from coming to his aid. He saw the man lying there in agony, and allowed himself to be profoundly moved by his suffering. He had an inward quality, which made him sympathetic to others, and which the pain of someone in distress could trigger off in him. But there was more to it than that; he felt the need to help too. He was genuinely kind, and sensitive towards the plight of others – something which the Bible recommends: "Be mindful of prisoners as if sharing their imprisonment, and of the ill-treated as of yourselves" (Heb 13.3). It wasn't simply the thought that he himself could readily be in the same situation which made him so concerned, but it was enough for him that another was suffering. This was something that he should try to remedy. When the Israelites were enduring grave hardships in Egypt, the Almighty reacted saying: "I have seen the affliction of my people in Egypt and have heard their cry because of their taskmasters; I know their sufferings, and I have come down to deliver them out of the hand of the Egyptians, and to bring them out of that land to a good and broad land, a land flowing with milk and honey" (Ex 3. 7-8). God heard, saw, knew and planned a liberating strategy. The Samaritan too saw the man lying in anguish by the wayside, heard inwardly his cry and grasped what he was suffering. His whole being opened up to the wounded one, and he set about being helpful.

He drew near to him, feeling a summons to behave responsibly. He did what he could immediately, pouring oil and wine into the wounds (the best indication that the Samaritan is Christ!). He was fortunate to have these commodities with him – yet we always have something to give! But he went further: he brought the man to an inn, so that he could rest and be treated there. He gave money to the innkeeper and undertook to pay the expenses for the ailing man. In brief, the Samaritan did all he could to completely cure the wounded one. He forgot about himself and his wealth, and devoted himself fully to the other. In this he was like Christ, who left his glory with his Father and gave himself to death for others.

Why Basically We Have To Help

All who belong to Christ form one body with him. "For just as the body is one and has many members ... so it is with Christ. For by one Spirit we are all baptized into one body" (1 Cor 12, 12, 13). "As it is, there are many parts, yet one body" (1 Cor 12.20). "But God has so composed the body, giving the greater honour to the inferior part, that there may be no discord in the body, but that the members may have the same care for one another. If one member suffers, all suffer together; if one member is honoured, all rejoice together" (1 Cor 12, 25-26). Both the joys and sorrows of others are in reality ours too. Their sufferings should mean that we in some way are affected. The hand cannot remain undisturbed, if the eye or ear is in pain. The greater the distress in a particular area of the body, the more pressing is the need for the other parts of it to be supportive. Likewise the acute difficulties of the weakest members of Christ's body, make very deserving demands on those who are healthier and more secure. We have to assist them as far as we can, especially those who cross our path. We can't be genuinely indifferent to the pleas of the suffering for help.

The Demands Are Vast

Of course, the needs of the neighbour are immense and of various kinds, and as a result the requests to us for help are numerous. If we allow these problems to touch us, they set enormous challenges before us. Such difficulties are so huge, especially when considered on a global or worldly scale, that in the face of them we feel useless and powerless – unable to do anything worthwhile! We realize that any efforts we make can only be like a stone thrown into an ocean. We might even think that we could achieve most by prayer and good-living, hoping that God's grace would accomplish the rest! Yet there has to be giving on our part. Our faith should assure us that our small contributions can be expanded by God's providence, and bear fruit beyond what we can imagine. The little we do gains great momentum, when it enters into the sweep and power of God's effective love. We too easily and erringly undervalue the significance of what we do!

In Attractive And Unattractive Situations

Sometimes an individual is asked or drawn to help another who is attractive and pleasant to deal with. Then in return the giver receives warm love and affection – which is most satisfying. The Almighty at times sets easy and fulfilling tasks before us – so enabling us to experience comforting contentment. For example, a charming person may approach us, seeking help or advice, and reveal rich experiences of life and a noble soul – while at the same time honouring us by having such trust in us. The encounter may prove greatly beneficial. Then our confidence is boosted, and we feel that we are of value. The mutual dialogue may even be inspirational.

We may wonder why people enter our lives for short periods – calling us to relate to them in some way, and then they vanish. Yet such brief encounters are never purely accidental – being planned by divine Providence. They are focuses set clearly before us, towards which we ought to direct our charitable intentions. These are faces given to us, whom we are summoned to love in more than a passing manner – through our prayer! We may be needed to give them a face from this side before God – to present them in our love before him. Our prayer becomes very alive and fruitful, when we avail of it as a way of fostering spiritual friendships and hiddenly doing good to others. God sends new people across our path, in order that we may expand the conscious reach of our love. Our spiritual acquaintances enable us to spread our influence afar.

However, the neighbour who seriously calls for our attention may be far from appealing – being rough, unsightly or ugly, and even awkward in manner and behaviour. Such a troublesome person may cause us annoyance by making persistent demands, and may prove to be a long-lasting nuisance or burden. Yet we cannot choose the people that we have to love or show charity to. Assisting them, in a kind and patient way, can be most difficult – even a form of crucifixion. Still the goodness of the other, however buried in layers of toughness and dullness, should eventually break through and bring us a surprising compensation for our diligent efforts. Through generous and tedious activity, we can acquire a surprising sense of how grace and the cross are present together. No help given to a needy person is ever entirely one-sided! God sees to it that blessings and benefits come to the benefactor too.

Loving Enemies

The NT (or more so the sweep of divine love) demands this. It tells us how to treat our foes. "Love your enemies, do good to those who hate you, bless those who curse you, pray for those who mistreat you" (6.27). This may be very contrary to how we naturally feel. We might prefer to make them pay for the harm they have done us – they shouldn't escape scot-free! We may not deliberately go out to avenge ourselves on them – though this does happen – but we can subtly mistreat them by being indifferent to and ignoring them – keeping out of their way, as far as possible. In this manner, we show our independence of and superiority over them, and make them feel that they have at least lost us.

There is no need for us to try to foster a close friendship with someone who for some reason has rejected us – at least to a degree. Friendship usually has to run smoothly to develop satisfactorily. Once its rhythm is broken, it can't easily be put on track again! We are not required to re-give ourselves emotionally to those, with whom we tried to be friends and failed. We may not have the enthusiasm to resume such a friendship, seeing that it did not work out for us in the past. In fact we may see God's providence at work in the separation that occurred. But we have to free ourselves from any hostile attitude towards lost friends, and in our inner hearts wish them well, and rejoice, when they are successful. Life goes on, and we frequently get to know other people, and continue on with our lives. But we have at least to be courteous and open to these former acquaintances – particularly so if they appear to have changed. A future acquaintance, if not friendship, may still be possible. Love always calls us to be creative. Our attraction for a former friend may be shaken, but we ought not maintain a permanently cold attitude towards such a one. Love never excludes fresh inspiration, change and new beginnings.

The problem may be very complicated, when a third person has got in the way and turned a friend away from us. We are then deprived of an acquaintance, because the freedom of another has worked against us. We are left dealing with two people instead of one. The person we liked may have been manipulated or in some way pressurised to move away from us, and we have to make allowances for this. Again no enmity should arise. We have to accept that losing friends is part of life. And where one is lost, there are others to be gained. There is no reason to be resentful! We should be above such losses, aware that when we fail in one thing, we often win something bigger. We really have no option in this matter, but to go with the moves and skills of others, even if we have to count ourselves losers. But then who fails in the heart of another! Circumstances and choices may fail to kill an attraction already felt deeply. A temporary setback is not the end.

Many Neighbours

The neighbour may be anyone who exists – including those in purgatory.

We continue to wonder how is it possible to love so many and do good to them. The only feasible way is by staying close to Christ, living in him. He touches all for us, in the measure that we are dwelling in him. Our reach is enormous, when he acts with us.

11

Sin Blocking Love

Most people, if not all, have to a degree an awareness of the destructive force that evil of this kind is, since it weakens their lives and blocks their capacity to love. The sharper a person's religious sensitivity, the more acute this is. It ought to result from a positive vision of what life should be, viewed in the light of God. A sober sense of the negativity of wayward conduct is healthy and sound, when it arises in the right context – that is from an appreciation of the Almighty, his love, beauty and goodness, and from the realization of not living adequately in harmony with him. Wickedness does not fit in with the deepest thrust of human existence – to be pleasing to the Creator and to treat all others well. It is, then, in part mysterious, as it has to be estimated against the brightness and marvel of God.

It can more specifically be described in various ways: a refusal to love the Lord or to submit to him; not allowing the force of his splendour, generosity and light to hold fitting sway in one's life. It means not accepting the limitations of being a creature, indebted to the Lord in all, and therefore thankful to him. It is a failure to recognize his supremacy – he who should be the master of the work of his own hands. It can rightly be viewed as not living in accordance with God's wishes – trying to go one's way independently of him. In brief, it amounts to not sufficiently acknowledging nor submitting to the Almighty. In its concrete reality, it may involve not having sufficient respect for the neighbour.

The eternal Master creates all in his own image and likeness (Gen 1.26). The Bible, however, never clarifies what exactly this means. In general it can be said that there is a profound resemblance to God in each one, and that it marks the whole person. It may convey the notion that each individual shares in basic characteristics of God, such as his freedom, his creative power, and intelligence. Above all, it indicates that there is a power in them, directing them to the Creator. The force of the Almighty is present there. He wants each of us to live like him in sanctity: "Be holy, for I, the Lord your God, am holy" (Lev 19.2). Going with such divine force means that human lives are being brightened with divine glory and beauty. Sin interferes with this process, by blocking the power and influence of the Lord, though this can never totally happen. Yet it can occur to an alarming degree.

Once people are not basically open to the Creator, they lose the guidance and clear direction that their lives should take, and as a result become spiritually dull and deviant. Then individuals turn too much to creatures and earthly things for the satisfactions they require, without paying attention to the Lord's salutary warnings against doing this. They easily flounder in short-term activities or wander in unfruitful areas. The resultant whirlwind of haphazard and confused behaviour is observable in the promiscuous lover, who moves from partner to partner, satisfying immediate wants, but finding no lasting peace. In this state, each is a person without proper focus, floundering about. This situation, of course, may change. Little ability is needed to be a great sinner.

Sin is not simply a personal matter, and can never be kept that way. It always affects others, and so exists in groups, and even in societies and cultures. When it is present in these latter, it can readily be accepted as normal or as a fitting way of life. Yet no matter where or how it lingers, it can't completely hide its ugly head. It is a negative force which never remains inactive. It frequently leads to much suffering! It is the greatest and most universal enemy of love. It is a strange reality – enticing and promising, yet damaging and disappointing.

There are two wonderful descriptions in the Bible of the process and consequences of sin. They show it in its true light – especially revealing its deception and the havoc it brings about. These compositions are masterpieces as regards the psychology of the sinner.

Genesis 3

In the beginning, God placed Adam and Eve in a garden filled with abundance, but gave them one very serious command – not to eat of the tree of knowledge of good and evil (Gen 2.17) – in order to show clearly to them their dependence on him. Left to themselves, they might have obeyed! – but a forceful temptation, prompted from outside, assailed them. The serpent, a symbol of wickedness or the devil, set about destroying the word of God already planted in them. He was very astute and cast doubt on the Lord's command, saying: "Did God (really) say, 'You shall not eat from any tree in the garden?'" – implying that their grasp of what was said might have been mistaken. The woman's response showed that she had lost the clarity and definiteness of the divine order. (I am not evaluating the role of male and female here, just showing how any of us can fall into sin). She repeated what God wanted, but with noteworthy changes. God is no longer called Lord, while the tree of the knowledge of good and evil becomes the one in the midst of the garden – so nothing special. She made known too that the threat of death was hanging over them, and that it would become a reality for them, if they disobeyed. She was worried and ill at ease. Because of her fear, she made the command stricter than it was (making doubly sure), adding that the particular tree should not even be touched. By altering God's clear instruction, she indicated that she had became mentally confused and had lost the simplicity of approach that was needed. Further influence from outside would make her both bewildered and vulnerable.

There is a lie involved in every sin – which is the acting out of a wrong viewpoint. The serpent bluntly, yet persuasively, read the situation falsely for her, claiming, "You shall not die" – and was believed. He claimed that the Creator had been too strict with them. This in a way implied that the basic problem was God himself, who was acting defensively, fearing that his creatures would become too free and independent – something that was within their right now and capacity! In other words, he had given them more than he realized, and he wasn't at ease with the new situation, and had to place curbs on them. He left himself in a vulnerable situation, and as a result was acting tyrannically! So Eve could rightly expose and discover his bluff. The image of the Almighty in Eve was thus greatly tarnished.

With a growing realization that she was wrongly placed in a false and unfair position and with the persistent feeling of being unduly deprived, the woman concentrated all the more on the small forbidden fruit, which was there within her reach. She viewed it solely from a human point of view, considering it both attractive and important. The tree was beneficial, offering good food, was pleasing to the eyes (beauty deceives many), and could bring about a new experience for her, as she asserted her independence. The fruit was observed wholly in relation to her, while the Creator's outlook was ignored. She was obsessed with one issue, while at the same time she was forgetting God's other known goodness and wisdom. Sin comes about, when the proper, full vision of reality is lost, and too much significance is given to one, often small aspect of it. The sinner feels that a tension can be eliminated by erring – perhaps just one time! – and then peace is possible in the future! An inflated, burning desire and a wrong evaluation of things lead to sin – which can be an effort to secure a calm future!

The sinful act is frequently very brief, like killing a person – yet with enormous consequences, some of which are felt immediately afterwards, and expressed in the lament: "What have I done? Or why did I do it?". The wrongdoing in this incident happened very quickly: "She took some of the fruit and ate it". The sinner likes to draw others into the wrongdoing! "She also gave some to her husband … and he ate". His resistance was equally weak, and he yielded easily to the woman's persuasion – perhaps a universal experience!

After sinning, when the emotional pressure has vanished, those guilty realize the deception in sin's empty promise. Adam and Eve immediately became aware that they had failed, were disobedient and had lost their dignity. They felt small and ashamed. In such a condition, their nakedness, without the protection of their uprightness, disturbed them and made them seem lowly. They turned in on themselves. Their sin made them less open, and they were afraid. Their calm approach to living and the ease they had with themselves were shattered. They felt distant from God too. They had lost the clarity and sureness that he gave them, and experienced confusion and guilt.

Later when the man and his wife heard God walking in the garden, they hid themselves among the trees. Sinners feel uncomfortable in the divine presence, and they, unless moved to a conversion, try to avoid meeting him. But the Almighty, in his loving mercy, sought them. He did not greet Adam and Eve by name – that was left for Christ to do later! – but called out, "Where are you?". He showed straightaway that he was concerned about them. Adam, now taking over from Eve the main role, replied that he hid himself because of his nakedness – which was not the main reason. God tried to evoke a clear admission of sin from them, but they were unable to do that. Neither of the two confessed directly that they had disobeyed, and so assumed responsibility for what they had done, but tried to excuse themselves. The man blamed the woman, while she in turn considered the serpent to be the culprit. They were as yet unable to say honestly, "We have done wrong" – more or less claiming that it wasn't really they themselves that failed, but that the pressure on them was too great.

The negative results of their one offence were enormous – showing how devastating a serious sin is. It is like as when a part of a well constructed machine goes wrong, and upsets the whole mechanism. The serpent was declared cursed, but yet a redeemer was promised, to eventually crush his power. Sin and the havoc it wrecks will later, through the divine mercy, be mastered and atoned for. Penalties were placed on both the woman and the man: pain in childbirth on the woman and having to be subject to her husband, if this has any meaning nowadays! One wonders is having children regarded here as her most important task! The man is punished too, having to endure hard work, toiling in ground that has been cursed, and so rough, with thorns and thistles. Finally he has to face death – as the woman too. It all amounts to an enormous reprimand for just one serious blunder! At times, we may question how could one sin bring about so much harm.

God saw to it that Adam and Eve could not eat any further of the fruit of that particular tree – they had already done enough damage. They were banned from the garden, from the place of their sin and their former way of life. Before doing so, the Lord restored some dignity to them, making garments of skin for them. He wished that their dignity be to some degree restored. His clothing them in this way was a prelude to his later adorning all with grace.

Adam and Eve ruined the attractive and bright future they had, and had to face a difficult, weary existence. Sin ever makes the path forward harder. The fact of being expelled from the garden makes clear what is lost by wickedness. Yet however strenuous the new way may be, it is directed by Providence, and in the long run, strangely enough, is the better one!

There is much spiritual wisdom about temptation and sin conveyed in this chapter. Wickedness is easy to accomplish, but causes enormous even mysterious devastation – to an extent that we grossly underestimate. But, thanks to Christ's death and resurrection, evil, in all its facets, is assailed by love, which overcomes it.

The Prodigal Son (Lk 15. 11-32)

The parable as originally told may have dealt with the fate of two peoples, the Gentiles and Israel. But pious tradition has tended to take it in a more individualistic manner – illustrating the adventures of a wild youth, who follows the impulses of his nature. However, some with good reason think that the emphasis is on the father, and that the story should be called "the parable of the merciful father".

According to the narrative, the younger of two brothers, showing initiative and a daring spirit, asked his father for his share of the family inheritance. He wanted this, so that he could live as his inclinations drove him. His parent, displaying a generous, liberal side, yielded to his request – perhaps thinking that the new responsibility would be good for his offspring! He would have a chance to show his abilities and creativity, and hopefully make good! Not many days afterwards, the young man, with adequate money in his pocket, went away to a foreign country, where he was unknown and could do as he wished. He wanted freedom, adventure and an enjoyable time – all of which he obtained for a period, but at a high price. He wasted his money, living a dissolute life. God's blessings and gifts should rather be used for a constructive purpose – in this way offering thanks to the Creator.

Sinners are content with the enjoyment of the moment or hour, and ignore or think far too little on what may happen in the future. They always risk, trusting in their own good fortune. The wisdom that the Bible offers doesn't impinge on them. They don't entertain its advice. "There is a way that seems right to a man, but its end is the way of death" (Prov 14.12). "The wicked falls by his own wickedness" (Prov 11.5). "The Lord is a stronghold to him whose way is upright, but destruction to evildoers" (Prov 10.29). But, alas, such sound warnings at times don't strike home. "Wisdom is too high for a fool" (Prov 24.7). The prodigal son needed no advice at this stage. Still God has his own ways of bringing sinners to their senses. "A fall to the ground is less sudden than a slip of the tongue/ that is why the downfall of the wicked comes so quickly" (Sir 20.17). The wicked often get caught in or run into adverse currents, which unfortunately flow against them at the wrong time. In this case, a famine arose in that land, and the young man found himself in dire need. He was willing to do the most menial of tasks and eat the crudest of food, but, alas, he could only obtain this by stealing. The sinner is often deserted by others, who distance themselves from him, when perhaps he needs most their support. The young man was left alone and unaided, in dire poverty. His fortune had changed drastically – yet he had brought that reversal on himself. The bright promise he had of a happy life ended dismally.

In this situation, what could the straying son do? He could opt for a life of crime, and try to survive by robbing others. But luckily enough he had no inclination for that. There was goodness deep within him, which perhaps he had acquired in his father's home, and which saved him from further wickedness. He had discovered an "empty tomb" in his own existence, and felt that this would have to be positively filled in. He got in touch with his deeper and better self, and realized that he should seriously and carefully examine his situation. He looked with realistic eyes at his present and previous life. He sharply noted that the servants who worked for his father were better off than he was. He too would be in a better state, if he were one of them. Though he considered that he had failed completely as a son, he humbly felt that he could at least seek a job as a workman in his former home.

He rightly grasped that his rehabilitation, even to some extent, depended more on the goodness of another, his father, than on himself. He could rely on his parent's uprightness and kindness, as he planned to make a deal with him. He decided, then, to return home in a humble, confessing attitude, saying openly: "I have sinned against heaven and before you; I am not worthy to be called your son". (He was aware that sin is mainly an offence against God). He was vividly conscious that he was not doing so with honour and in triumphant success. Yet however battered and humiliated a person may be, it is always ennobling to make the right decision and to move honestly even with shame towards the way of reform. (The fact that the father rather than the mother is mentioned is strange in Jewish culture, where a son counts so much for a mother! Obviously there is a theological message in this).

Many consider that the behaviour of the father is what is dominant in the parable. Even though the son abandoned him, the old man himself never did so as regards his offspring. He lived always awaiting the return of his loved one – being ever in a state of expectancy and very eager to see and meet him. When he saw him coming, he ran to welcome him and greeted him with great joy and love. For the father, his son had been no better than dead, but now he was happily alive. He had been lost and was found. This parent celebrated his erring son's homecoming with magnanimity and joyful enthusiasm. No words of bitterness or disappointment were spoken. This warm-hearted man did not react, saying, "You've had your chance; from now on look after yourself". He wished rather to let his own bigness and generosity be dominant – allowing forgiving love and delight to hold sway. He must have thought that surely his son would respond favourably to the strength of his love. He wanted the past to be forgotten, and a new era to begin. Love that pardons lets old grievances and disappointments go, and allows the other to start again. It looks at the deeper side of the guilty person – the part that so far has been dormant and neglected. It encourages change and creativity in another.

The elder son was not pleased with his father's approach. He thought that his behaviour had gone too far – that he had lost balance, making too much out of his son, who had erred and needed to be punished! He had been loyal and diligent all his days, and his parent never made any celebration for him. Perhaps he never asked for it. Much less, he reckoned, should be given to his brother! He viewed things totally from his own limited outlook and experience. He was rigidly tied to his ideas of justice and counterbalance. He wasn't open to the originality and newness that go with a richer dimension of love than he had. He was a prisoner of his own isolation and loneliness. He wasn't able at all to cope with the surprises that can come from a loving person.

He did not realize that errors and sins bring out a higher facet of love, both in God and in those who are blessed by his grace. The elder son was well treated at home, receiving enough there, but always within the routine of the normal. This was fitting and adequate, since his own wooden personality and his moderate capabilities did not call for or demand more. Yet he wanted others to be treated in the same way. He desired to control his father, in his dealings with the younger son, and was annoyed that he did not act according to his (the son's) viewpoint. He was locked in his thinking to his own limited world. He was a good, but not very open, person, who failed to see that others can have far finer gifts than he had. The wayward son was more flexible, and had greater impulses towards love than his brother, though for a period he was unable to restrain and direct them wisely. When his reckless adventures brought him to ruin, the depths of his misery luckily led him to discover the marvel of his father's love, which opened up a new vision of that same for him. It is important for us to recognize that sinners may draw out the best from others and especially from God. The need to forgive is ever there.

God's Great Mercy

The Creator is always searching for sinners, those erring and straying – trying to enlighten them and bring them to share in his life or love. Jesus expressed this same idea: "I have other sheep that do not belong to this fold. I must bring them also, and they will listen to my voice. So that there will be one flock and one shepherd" (Jn 10.16).

As has already been stated, God's great mercy and love are shown above all in his death and resurrection. Since Christ endured so much for us, who can doubt the seriousness of his concern to pardon all! The most hardened and wickedest of sinners can scarcely resist the might of such generosity! The divine capacity to pardon is greater than all human evil. The psalmist assures us of this: "If you, O Lord, should mark iniquities, Lord, who could stand? But there is forgiveness with you. ... For with the Lord there is steadfast love, and with him is great power to redeem" (Ps 130. 3,4,7). No matter how sinfully burdened a person may feel, the Creator's kindness and willingness to forgive is immensely consoling. "Whenever our hearts condemn us, God is greater than our hearts" (1 Jn 3.20).

12

The Holy Spirit And Love

The very mention of the Holy Spirit sets us thinking on love and life – both being the same in God. We picture him as having an abundance of or overflowing with these. We hold that he can readily share such loving vitality with us – so making our lives, to a degree, similar to his own. He is rightly called, in a well-known hymn, "the giver of gifts". We speak of him too as "the Lord, the Giver of life". "The Spirit gives life" (Jn 6.63). He is also presented as the holy Spirit (Lk 1.35). The psalmist can rightly make this request to God: " Put a new and right spirit within me … and take not thy holy Spirit from me" (Ps 51. 10,11). We sense that, if we could open ourselves completely to him, our existences would be very contented and fruitful. By paying more attention to him, our lives would be changed enormously, and we would become wiser and more achieving! We would even find great possibilities for doing good! We would then be given many blessings and would grow rich in love. But, alas, we may not be sufficiently prepared for, nor ready to receive, to a fitting degree, his mighty power. As a result, we are all the poorer and less adorned.

Yet our thinking in his regard has to move beyond ourselves. The Spirit is the vitality of life or love between the Father and the Son – which is so great as to be the third person of the Blessed Trinity. So we can rightly bow before the mystery of his greatness, while still knowing that we are worshipping the one, true God. Every action of his is marked by his divine magnificence and power. What he gives or advises always springs from God's goodness and wisdom. Any gift or benefit bestowed on us by him means that our existences are enlivened and brightened by the enormous force of his grandeur.

The Depths Of God

The Spirit is the accomplishing side of the Almighty. According to St Basil, it is he who brings about all things. He was present at the work of creation as well as at that of redemption. In the OT, the Spirit of God is the divine power at work in the world – creating and sanctifying. But the same writing foresees a future more important outpouring of the Spirit (Ez 36. 26-29; Jl 3. 1-5), leading to greater holiness and more wonderful activity. The more we see the force of the Spirit at work in the world, the wiser and more open we become.

The NT presents the Spirit in relation to God to us in many ways. According to John's gospel, he makes Christ's message, which is that of the Father, fully known. St. Paul says that he is the One who really understands the Almighty. The Spirit knows the depths of God (1 Cor 2.10) – his mysterious wonder. He experiences fully in a lived manner what the divine existence, in all its aspects, is. He is totally at one with everything divine – God's supreme life, holiness, power and wisdom – while yet having his own personal distinction.

The Creator in his mystery excels all that we can know about him. His greatness, majesty and glory are infinitely beyond what the human mind can grasp. But through his revelation and the help of the Spirit, we are able to catch a glimmer of his splendour. This latter leads us to repect the profundity of God and his ways, and to maintain our lives directed towards him. When we read passages from the OT, which proclaim the grandeur of the Creator, the Spirit sharpens our dull hearts to embrace him with wonder and appreciation. He moves us too to be in awe and reverence before him, as we say: "Honour and majesty are before him; strength and beauty are in his sanctuary" (Ps 96.6). We are inspired too to offer him praise and thanks: "For great is the Lord, and greatly to be praised" (Ps 96.4). "I will give thanks to thee, O Lord and King, and will praise thee as God my Saviour. I will give thanks to thy name, for thou hast been my protector and helper and hast delivered my body from destruction …" (Sir 51.1-2).

The more we admire God, the further our own dignity is exalted, and the greater our lives become. We grasp him in the measure that we love him – that is in so far as we allow the Spirit to warm our indifferent hearts. He has to dispose and help us, so that we have deep contact with the Father and the Son.

Being With Christ And Bringing Him To Others

The Spirit knows Christ completely and intimately, as he does the Father – being the vitality between both. He accompanied Jesus at every stage, while he, the bringer of salvation, was on earth. He was with him – "The Spirit remained on him" (Jn 1.32) – helping him to live in total obedience to the Father. He guided the Son, as he went about doing good (Acts 10.38), giving joy to many (Lk 2.10). He was markedly with him in his death and resurrection. The words he spoke carry the force of the Spirit: "The words that I have spoken to you are spirit and life" (Jn 6.63). Jesus presents himself as the source of the Spirit: "He who believes in me, as the Scripture has said, 'Out of his (her too) heart shall flow rivers of running water'" (Jn 7.38). These flow from the pierced side of Jesus – and are a description of the Spirit that is given. This happens, when the risen Christ, to whom all power has been given, at the Father's side, pours out the Spirit. He, the third Person of the Blessed Trinity, fulfils through the Son that which the Father desires. The Son makes all one body, of which he is the head. But he does so in conjunction with the Spirit, who imparts to each the fullness of deity in a unique and personal way. Jesus unifies, but the Spirit diversifies! – yet it's all one work.

Christ and the Spirit work fully in unison. What Jesus does, the Spirit likewise is involved in. The NT does not adequately distinguish between them, stating : "Now the Lord is the Spirit". Both enable us to share in and benefit from Christ's salvific work. The Spirit is the power and voice of Jesus present in us! This person of the Blessed Trinity remains very anonymous and humble, as he almost says: "Get to know Jesus and be at one with him, not me". He is ever making the Son known, a role Jesus proclaimed: "He will bear witness to me" (Jn 15.26). He does not convey other than the Son's teaching: "He will take what is mine and declare it to you" (Jn 16.15). He is ever active in those in whom he dwells making Jesus better understood and more alive in them. And he does so to a large extent from within.

The Spirit, as the light of Christ, shows up what is false and valuable in life: "And when he comes, he will convince the world concerning sin and righteousness and judgement: concerning sin, because they do not believe in me; concerning righteousness, because I go to the Father, and you will see me no more; concerning judgement, because the ruler of the world is judged" (Jn 16.8-11). The basic sin is not to believe in the Son of God, and the Spirit makes clear the consequences of this error. Righteousness is Jesus' going to the Father, and living correctly is moving in faith with him in the same direction. Judgement has to be seen in a more hopeful perspective, because a power greater than all the forces of evil is at work in the world. In brief, the Spirit brings home to us the wickedness of sin, and the wonder of Christ's salvific activity for all.

In The Christian Life

God, the Father, forms all, as he adorns them in numerous ways – yet always in conjunction with the Son's redeeming work and the action of the Spirit. So Paul can write: "We are his handiwork" (Eph 2.10). The Father

conforms us to the image of his Son (Rom 8.29) – a wonderful development brought about by the Holy Spirit (Rom 8.9).

The fact that we are led by the Spirit means that we are sons of God:
"For all who are led by the Spirit are sons of God" (Rom 8.14). Sonship
means sharing in Christ's special relationship with his Father, and so being
most intimate with him. "You received a spirit of sonship, in which we cry
'Abba', Father" (Rom 8.15). Both male and female can have this sonship
in different ways! Paul describes this marvellous situation as follows:
"God made us alive together with Christ (by grace you have been saved),
and raised us up with him, and made us sit with him, in the heavenly
places in Christ Jesus" (Eph 2.4-6). Heavenly life is begun here on earth,
as an initial stage of a far more total transformation.

We tend to fail to fittingly appreciate the wonder of our Christian existence. The NT mentions that we are in Christ: "As therefore you received
Christ Jesus the Lord, so live in him" (Col 2.6). But it also states that we
are in the Spirit: "You are in the Spirit, if the Spirit of God dwells in you"
(Rom 8.9). The reality for us is one and the same. If we are so blessed, we
are continually being uplifted, because the spirit of the one who raised
Jesus from the dead dwells in us. (Rom 8.11). He has Christ's generosity
– that of the one who died for all (2 Cor 5.14). He, in turn, makes us self-
sacrificing like Jesus. His influence on our lives can be without measure,
as he ever tries to make us more loving. The Spirit makes us free in the
fullest sense. "Where the Spirit of the Lord is, there is freedom" (2 Cor
4.17). He gives each of us, in the circumstances we're in, the capacity to
make choices in accordance with God's love, and so to respond to him in
whatever way the Almighty summons. He likewise assists people to dis-
entangle themselves, when caught in unwholesome situations, but they
have to cooperate with him. Liberated individuals give as much scope as
possible to Jesus in their lives and can say with St Paul, "I live, no longer
I, but Christ lives in me" (Gal 2.20). The freedom that is offered is an open
path to serve God and others. Sin puts barriers across this way, and is to
be avoided. No wonder this advice is given: "For sin is not to have power
over you, since you are … under grace" (Rom 6.14).

The Flesh And The Spirit

The struggle between the flesh and the spirit is not only an important theme
in the writings of St Paul, but it is a major issue in the life of every individual. The human person is made up of two conflicting forces, the flesh
and the spirit. Each of these strives to gain the upper hand. The flesh is the
more aggressive of the two and works towards the elimination of the spirit!
The latter does not seek to get rid of the other, but aims at controlling its

tendencies and directing them towards good. Flesh for the apostle is the drive in all to follow their natural desires and inclinations, as they wish, and to try to develop fully by their own efforts and abilities. It amounts to attempting to live without Christ and the benefits of his salvific work. Efforts to be self-sufficient and independent show up one side of the human make-up. There are in a sense two personalities in everyone – the spiritual and the fleshy.

The Christian vocation is to give way to the spiritual gifts and callings on offer. This is required in order to find the nobility that individual lives ought to rise to. But this may become a reality only through struggle. The two orientations of the flesh and the spirit are contrary to each other: "For those who live according to the flesh are concerned with the things of the flesh, but those who live according to the spirit with the things of the spirit. ... For the concern of the flesh is hostility towards God" (Rom 8.5,7). Both these drives are very deep-rooted in each person. What the Son and the Spirit offer is spiritual: "And as is the man of heaven, so are those who are of heaven" (1 Cor 15.48).

Trying to direct spiritually human desires or making them be at the service of love is not easy, and can't be done without the help of the Holy Spirit. This must be sought and prayed for. It is only given in the context of a commitment to Christ (however vague), and is achieved at a price: "Those who are in Christ Jesus have crucified the flesh and its desires" (Gal 5.24). The inward war may be difficult.

A Taste For Spiritual Things

Whenever people, be they Christian or not, have a taste for religion, the Holy Spirit is at work in them. However, they may not realize that he is involved in what is taking place. The Christian is very aware of his activity. He creates in believers an inner sensitivity for spiritual realities and values.

Many wonder how this is acquired or how they can pass it on to others. The NT describes what is involved. Those who appreciate the Christian belief are "those who have been enlightened, who have tasted the heavenly gift, and have become partakers of the Holy Spirit, and have tasted the goodness of the world to come and the powers of the age to come" (Heb 6.4). In order to be sufficiently religiously tuned or turned on, there is need for enlightenment (instruction and inward light). The question arises then for the missionary minded person, "How can I help in bringing this gift to another?" or "Is it possible to do so?". The imparting of knowledge is a help, but a spiritual feel for its beauty and dignity is needed too, something the Spirit alone can provide.

A vivid sensitivity for what lies ahead (the future marvel that awaits us beyond death) and a felt urgency to attain it are required, in order to become a believer. With this goes the realization that this world is passing rapidly, which in itself favours serious thought. As regards this matter, the Spirit is quietly creative, awakening and broadening the human heart, and drawing it towards an other-worldly outlook.

He too encourages and enables us to apppreciate God's blessings. He is from God, given "that we might understand the gifts bestowed on us by God" (1 Cor 2.12) – especially Christ's activity and teaching. The person that listens to the Spirit has a deep appreciation of the Son and his work.

When people fail to grasp the importance of religion or aspects of belief, they show that they need a different interior sensitivity. Their hearts have to be touched in a new way. A Russian spiritual writer, St. Seraphim of Sarov, notes this clearly: "God is a fire which warms and kindles our hearts. If we feel in our hearts the cold which comes from the devil – for the devil is cold – let us pray to the Lord and he will come and warm our hearts with love for our neighbour. And before the warmth of his face, the cold of the enemy will be put to flight". The Holy Spirit does this, as a well-known hymn indicates: "Warm what is frozen in us".

The Gifts Of The Spirit

Divine love is infinitely rich, with countless blessings to offer. These are shared out by the Creator, through the Spirit, in various manners and degrees – no two being blessed in a totally equal manner! Yet each individual receives enough benefits from him – some that others have, but also special and individual ones. All should use thankfully what has been allotted to them and be content with this. "Having gifts that differ according to the grace given to us, let us use them" (Rom 12. 6). There is no need to be jealous of others, envying what is granted to them. True contentment is found in accepting oneself as one is, with the measure of talents that one has. The Spirit has a part to play in bringing about such genuineness.

"There are different kinds of spiritual gifts but the same spirit" (1 Cor 12.4). They all manifest the richness and excellence of the Almighty. They are Christ-like qualities, which were always evident in the Son's life, while he was on earth. Isaiah mentions six gifts of the Spirit, while some texts of the Bible add a seventh, piety. These strengthen the life of faith, hope and charity. Faith is helped by understanding, knowledge and counsel; hope by the fear of God and by fortitude; charity by piety and wisdom – as Cardinal Martini has indicated. These blessings aid individuals to live out the Beatitudes. They assist us to be strong and faithful in a turbulent and contradictory world. Some people, for example, have spiritual knowledge, and are learned in spiritual matters; others understand God and his depths in a remarkable way, and know the ideas or words that best portray his mystery. There are still more who have wisdom, and are very sharp in recognizing and choosing the ways of God: they are skilled in the discernment of spirits. Their advice is very valuable. Yet again, some have the capacity to heal and to work miracles (cf 1 Cor 12.4-11) – having special creative powers. The Spirit distributes his gifts as he wishes, yet always for the common good. The greatest one he can bestow is the perfection of love, which means living, in the measure given, in line with his attractive, all embracing, and generous existence. This precious gift has many faces: "Love is patient, love is kind; it is not jealous. … It bears all things, believes all things, hopes all things, endures all things" (Cf 1 Cor 13.4-7). This description portrays a love that is divine! Those who live even to a degree in this manner ought to realize that they are on a very exalted plane.

Paul enumerates the fruits of the Spirit, which are evident in the lives of those in whom he dwells: "love, joy, peace, patience, kindness, goodness, faithfulness, meekness, self-control" (Gal 5.22,23). Each of us may now and again sense and appreciate the known goodness of some of these blessings, but, alas, we may be more often acutely aware that we lack them. Their presence was and is evident in the life of Jesus.

One title of the third Person of the Trinity, "the Consoler" (Jn 14.16) makes him especially dear to us. When there is anxiety and turmoil in our lives, the consolation he offers can make our disturbed state of soul and mind peaceful. As we well know, the journey of life is strewn with many pitfalls and difficulties, and often we are very weak. Yet in its many hard trials, none can be of greater assistance to us than the Spirit, in his role of Consoler.

St. John Damascene puts the significance of the Spirit vividly before us: "Spirit of God, direct, authoritative, the fountain of wisdom, and life and holiness; God existing and addressed along with the Father and the Son : uncreated, full, creative, all-ruling, all-effecting, all-powerful, of infinite power, Lord of all creation and not subject to any lord: deifying, not deified: filling, not filled: shared in, not sharing in: sanctifying, not sanctified". He can change and bless our lives in most remarkable ways.

13

Love and the Providence of God

When we look at our lives, while realizing that God is very concerned about us, we have to acknowledge that his providence has brought us this far – to where and how we are, at this particular time. It is not just by chance that we are in our present situation, be that satisfactory or not. No matter what kind it may be, we have good reason to be joyful and hopeful – though it may not come easily to us to feel so optimistic. The divine influence or thrust that has led us to our actual setting is, and has been, working for our good: "For you are just in all you have done; all your ways are faultless, all your ways right" (Dan 3.27). Our lives advance, with the Lord's goodness and sureness having a profound bearing on them – even if this is hard to see. There is a sound motive behind all that happens to us. This fact is difficult to grasp, especially when we fear that it was our own errors that mainly brought us to where we are now!

If we could view ourselves with the gaze of the divine eyes or his wisdom, we might be surprised at how kind the Almighty is to us, and has been in the past. Only in his light can we assess our lot accurately. Often we fail in this, because we lack his clear vision. The lord in his wisdom sees our true picture, and we need his viewpoint to sharply evaluate our lives. "Whence then comes wisdom? ... God alone understands the way to it, and alone knows its place" (Jb 28. 20, 23). We require a sharing in this to understand ourselves well, and he readily grants it, to an adequate extent, to us. He "gives wisdom to the wise and knowledge to those who understand. He reveals deep and hidden things and knows what is in the darkness, for the light dwells with him" (Dan 2.21,22). However, we never know ourselves fully, and our existences remain partially in obscurity. In such circumstances, we have to trust in God's guiding providence – while showing deep respect for him. "Truly the fear of the Lord, that is wisdom, and to depart from evil is understanding" (Jb 28.28). The Bible makes plain that in God alone, in the fullest sense, is our hope, our peace and our understanding. We have to maintain faith in him and his guiding hand, come what may. We, in fact, learn much about the Almighty, by coming to terms with ourselves in the here and now. The deeper we can do this, the more enriching is our experience of him!

The Unifying Thread

While accepting that God's providence is governing our lives, we may wonder at times how do all the haphazard events that we have lived through fit together. Yet we rightly hold that we are stamped by everything we have done or that has happened to us. We realize that there is a centre in us, which registers them all, and from where they have at least an unconscious influence on us. Our past to some extent is contained in this inward storeroom. We know that a big part of our present personal wisdom springs from there – previously gained in the cut and thrust of living. We are aware that we would be truer to ourselves and stronger, if we could accept our former experiences more lovingly and joyfully, as part of our living selves, and live wisely out of them. God somehow is moulding us, as he wishes, through all such occurrences: "We are his work" (Eph 2.10). Shakespeare masterfully describes the process: "There is a divinity that shapes our ends, rough hew them how we will". Even if there have been numerous twists and turns in our history, some of them rather puzzling, and a countless host of unfinished happenings there (things begun and never ended, briefly endured acquaintances), a divine pattern is being weaved through and by them all. God's love directs each life, and that may be in the strangest of manners. The more outlandish and bewildering certain events and happenings may seem to us, the more the greatness of the Almighty may be active in them – something that eventually will be revealed to us!

Success Or Failure Not The Ultimate

Some feel very happy that their good fortune led them to where they now are. They can verify what Shakespeare said that "there is a tide in the affairs of men, which taken at the flood leads on to fortune". They availed fully of the opportunities on offer, and now they rank as successful. They enjoy, as a result, an abiding sense of contentment.

Many, alas, have a less satisfactory experience. Things haven't gone right for them. They may now lamentingly think that it was really their own mistakes that brought them to their present state and situation. They may have to recognize too that formerly they neglected God or ignored his commands and guidance, and that they paid dearly for their sins. Yet even in this, God's providence was at work. He may have had to allow their errors and transgressions to achieve what he wanted! Had things gone differently, they might have made even greater mistakes and be in a worse condition now! Their past states of mind could have led them further astray.

It takes courage and faith to recognize that the best position for each of us is the one in which we are now! The present hour, viewed correctly, ever invites us to read our existing situation in a favourable manner, even if we are more superficially inclined to think that it could scarcely be any worse. We tend to be preoccupied too much about what might have been! This does not mean that our existing behaviour and attitudes, and even the circumstances of our lives, don't have to be changed. But the process of correction will be embarked on serenely and pursued with hope and trust in the Almighty. Spiritual writings like de Caussade's book, *Self-Abandonment To Divine Providence*, can help us to see and accept our actual state correctly and to have a wholesome regard for our past performances. In all states of life satisfaction can be found.

A Wise Outlook

True living has to be in conformity with God's will, which must be warmly welcomed – both as it is in the here and now and as it has been in the past. (All quotations given here are from de Caussade's book). "We must not dictate to God's will, nor attempt to set limits to its action, for he is all powerful". "If what God himself selects for you does not suffice for you, what other hand can more satisfyingly serve you?". We are reacting against a current which we really cannot resist, if we don't go along with his desires! When we are frustrated by what is over and done with, aren't we foolishly regretting his plans for us, wishing that they were different! We cannot find inner harmony with such behaviour. "Do you expect to find peace by struggling against the Almighty?". Contentment is found solely in bending to him. We are clearly opposing the Almighty, when we are angry with ourselves for our mistakes and for our present circumstances!

The situation is different, however, when we make a lament to God and pray in this fashion: "Why, Lord, did you put me in this situation or allow me to fall into it? Why did you let me make these mistakes in the past?". Then we are dialoguing with the Creator, and striving to receive light and help from him.

The best we can do now is to accept fully what is gone – since it has shaped our present selves. "The past is myself, my own history, the seed of my present thoughts, the mould of my present disposition" (from R. L. Stevenson). It greatly contributes to our individuality and identity. No matter how trying our past situation may have been, or how distressful our present one is, they serve a very useful purpose. "The will of God has nothing but sweetness, favours, and treasures for souls submitted to it" –

a fact that we often don't sufficiently grasp! We have to read our actual state with positive eyes. It ever opens up new possibilities for us and presents us with areas along which we can develop and grow.

We need to search for God in everything that happens or has happened to us – see his hand or find traces of him in it. We should look at each event and say: "It is the Lord, and in all circumstances we should find a gift from God". The Lord sets us in places, where we can grow spiritually, along the lines he wishes. We can there cultivate certain qualities and virtues, which he considers good for us.

If we look carefully at our lives, we may become very conscious of our personal weaknesses, such as a lack of confidence, being shy or reserved. And yet these characteristics may have proved to be strong weapons in our favour and defences against very grave errors! The fact of being timid may have meant not taking daring and imprudent risks. Because we failed to achieve one thing, we may have been ready and free to undertake something better. There is nothing negative in life which, when properly dealt with, cannot produce good! All life's episodes can have positive effects. An apparently unpopular negative attitude in someone can arise from an unnoticed longing for something deeper than the ordinary! "Everything becomes bread to nourish me, soap to cleanse me, fire to purify me". There is a good and noble purpose, attached to all seemingly contrary vicissitudes. "Hold for certain that whatever happens to you internally and externally is for the best". There is great wisdom in having such a state of mind.

A Divine Work Of Art

Those who look at their existences with the eyes of faith consider it like a piece of canvas, on which God is fashioning a marvellous design. The Supreme Artist is, and has been, weaving and blending the various lines (often very crooked ones) and the different shades of colour together, to achieve the wonderful end product, which he alone can bring about. Portions of the whole work, especially when taken in isolation or out of context, may look bewildering or unattractive; yet they contribute to something magnificent – a creation of the almighty designer. All life's episodes have to be viewed as contributing to that noble pattern. They help to build up the splendour of an individual transformed in Christ.

When things occur or have taken place which leave individuals in dire straits, perhaps crushed in spirit or bearing a severe trial or cross, the loving hand of God may seem far distant. Deep belief is needed then, in order to recognize his presence in such dark periods. "The life of faith is nothing else than a continual pursuit of God through everything that disguises, misrepresents and, so to speak, destroys and annihilates him". The *Book*

Of Job is perhaps the most profound treatment there is on an individual struggling with God, who has become incomprehensible to him. In the end, Job is enlightened through further revelation and recognizes the greatness of the Almighty and his strange ways. "I know that thou canst do all things, and that no purpose of thine can be thwarted" (Job 42.20). Blind faith in the Lord has to be maintained in "the dark night" and hope preserved in his mighty power. The Lord can rapidly change situations: "For it is easy with the Lord suddenly, in an instant, to make a poor man rich" (Sir 11.21). When the Creator seems (or has seemed) to be distant, then strangely enough he is all the nearer! His mysterious greatness, which contains a dark side that we cannot fathom, is strongly touching our lives, when we are most puzzled by him. He may be leading us all the more, when we don't clearly sense his guidance. He may be more active in the unsuccessful life than in the successful one! He uses his ability to seem to be near or distant for his own purpose. Whatever way he chooses, it is always for our good.

Unknown

No one can grasp clearly or know in detail the intricate plan which is being carried out in the individual life. We don't know God, nor the world, nor even ourselves completely. We are on an adventure, and however ordinary and humdrum it may appear, it is directed towards a definite, worthwhile goal. It is impossible to calculate the value of particular incidents – details or twists on the explorer's or traveller's journey. What is mainly required is to give oneself to the Lord, without trying to understand everything. "Let us surrender ourselves to God, without working out vain and idle systems of sanctity". What is most significant is what is being achieved, not what is known. "Come not to know the map of spirituality, but to possess the land". "The way forward is into the unknown, and God alone is followed". "When you have neither map nor way nor wind nor river, then only can you make happy journeys". As long as we travel with the Lord, we have all the guidance that we need – though the course may be the hard one, where pure faith is needed. His sure hand works in manners that are not totally visible or revealed to us. This fits in with what the Bible says: "For as the heavens are higher than the earth, so are my ways higher than your ways and my thoughts than your thoughts" (Is 55.9).

In Goethe's *Faust* the Fates recognize the errors they have made, in terminating lives too haphazardly: "Useless lives dragged out their story, / Lingered on in light and breath, / But the hopes of youth and glory / She cut short with gloomy death". They did not always act wisely: "Yet I too, I'm bound to say, / Made mistakes in my own day, / So my shears are sheathed for surety / In the interests of security". Yet God and his loving wisdom lies behind the so-called errors of the Fates: "Does evil befall a city, unless the Lord has done it"? (Am 3.6).

Fragmentary Yet Unified

As individuals look back on their lives, their musings may take them to many places. Promptings of the sea or the sky, but more importantly of the Spirit may have driven them in wide and distant directions – yet there was always an element of mystery in their journeyings. Obviously the river or flow of their movements did not move in a straight course, but formed haphazard channels. They became actors – with different roles and stages. Seeds or ripples from their presence and achievements, however small they may have been, were scattered to the winds, and the full fruit that was eventually brought forth is not known to them. Hopefully it is significant!

As people make a general survey of their lives, they may wonder why a definite selection of people crossed their paths. No two have met exactly the same ones! Such persons encountered can be divided into categories: those worked with, travelled with, those who were friends, those briefly spoken to, those who helped, those seen or to whom an attraction was felt, but with whom there was no exchange of greetings, those who were near, and finally those to whom they did harm.

The impressions made on us by others remain to a large extent in the subconscious, and from there they help us in a creative manner! Their remembrance can brighten our imaginations and inspire dreams in us. But such people can become more real for and nearer to us, when we bring them into our prayers. When we come before God in thought and bear them in mind, we are presenting them to the Creator. Perhaps this is the only time that their name is echoed before his throne from our world. Through this pious exercise, we can maintain active and living contact with many, who otherwise would be more distant from us. Hopefully we do good to them and may even heal them from a distance. Being with them in prayer, we extend enormously the range of our concrete benevolence and foster friendships far and wide.

In general, by our prayer we can unify the many haphazard encounters and apparent casual happenings of our lives, pulling them all somehow together.

Owning Our Past With Joy

In our efforts to be fully ourselves, we may have to work especially hard at repossessing our past with joy. We need to bathe all there in the fountain of love. We have to recreate a new vision of what is gone or see it in a new light, and embrace it more sympathetically. This leads to a newly discovered contentment, and boosts our confidence and hope. Rather than be burdened with regrets, it is more fitting to humbly and courageously pardon ourselves – while making an effort at the same time to be better and wiser in the future. We ought, surely, to be kind and generous to ourselves! It is necessary to bring more to the fore, in our thinking, all the good that we have done, and in no way minimize our accomplishments. Those who strive to place their lives in the perspective of love are engaged in a noble task. With such an attitude it is easier to make full use of one's talents in the here and now, as a form of thanksgiving to the Almighty.

14

Prayer – A Meeting and Dialogue in Love

Writing on prayer has to be regarded as a daring and difficult undertaking. No matter how advanced we may seem to be at it, we are still only beginners, and have to keep in mind the words put by a disciple to Jesus, "Lord, teach us to pray" (Lk 11.1)! We remain always inept at it: "We do not know how to pray as we ought, but the Spirit himself intercedes for us with sighs too deep for words" (Rom 8.26). Every time we begin this spiritual exercise, we should realize how incapable we are of doing it well, and fittingly ask for the help of the Spirit. It is in this general context, of always adjusting better to prayer, that what is written here about it has to be set.

Prayer is the most conscious way we have of expressing our love for God, or offering a reverent response to him for his goodness to us. There are other ways in which we show our esteem for the Creator – by being open to him, living as he wills, accepting what he sends, meeting him in the sacraments and in others (especially in the poor) – though these activities are also forms of prayer viewed more widely. There is, however, something very special about prayer in the ordinary sense – that is when we deliberately and respectfully think about him! When we engage in this task, we turn, with full awareness, to the Almighty and to his greatness. We humbly bear in mind before whom we stand – recognizing his immensity which in every sense engulfs us. We are created in him, and in his reality we live and move and have our existences. In prayer, we take a stand where we mainly belong – in the outward sweep of God, and direct ourselves towards his divine might which both sustains and is beyond us. We acknowledge the all-surpassing richness of the Almighty. To pray means to be close to his mysterious wealth, in all its variety and splendour, and to be enriched by it. Then we are communicating with him, who is powerful beyond measure and who is extraordinarily bounteous. We are at our best, when we are doing so!

Prayer, then, is an awareness of being present before the excellence of God, and of being attentive to him, in an attitude of love. But more important for each of us is the fact that he is looking at us, showing interest in us, and eager to talk with and listen to us. He is there before us. Praying projects us outwardly to the Creator, whose eyes are on us. The person who does so withdraws mentally from all worldly matters, preoccupations and concerns, in order to concentrate on him, whose gaze is sensed. Prayer means being consciously before the Creator, whether just being with him, or adoring him, or praising him or asking requests of him. Such an activity is inspired from above, and is always an acceptance of his call, or summons or invitation.

This article favours a combination of two types of prayer – having a mystical approach to the Almighty, and with such an orientation drawing out the meaning of Christ's life and teaching. The biblical texts portray the inner life, activity, nobility, wisdom and power of the infinite Lord. He, in his immensity, is somehow present in them. The divine has to be grasped in the human.

Mystical Prayer

Many ancient religious writers, like Origen and Gregory of Nyssa, adopt a mystical attitude in their approach to God. They are mainly struck by the divine greatness and the fact that he is not fully knowable. He is infinite and mysterious. His brilliance or brightness is beyond what we can imagine or directly experience or tolerate. Before him, we are very poor and small. With such a realization, the need to bow down in adoration before his grandeur, and to admire and praise the marvel of his existence, is sensed.

Appreciating the Almighty's brilliance and worth is a most beneficial exercise for us; for flashes of his glory and power descend on us – often in an unconscious manner. Such divine sparkles bring us many spiritual blessings – wisdom, strength, love. In this encounter, of the creature with the Creator or the finite with the Infinite, the divine One bestows also a sharing in the serenity of his own inner life. He gives us enormous spiritual vitality towards living well and doing good.

True human beauty results from gazing at God's indescribable graciousness. Origen has written most fittingly about this: "The beloved (Christ) is called beautiful and attractive, and the more he will be observed with spiritual eyes, all the more beautiful and attractive he will appear. In fact not only will his look and beauty appear marvellous, but also a new beauty and a new marvellous look will come over the one who looks at and observes him". Such splendour enters first into the soul's inner depths. No wonder, then, that Peter exhorts women (and men too) to aim at interior adornment. "Let not yours be the outward adorning and braiding of hair, decoration of gold, and wearing of robes, but let it be the hidden person of the heart with the imperishable jewel of a gentle and quiet spirit, which in God's sight is very precious" (1 Pet 3.3,4). Gazing at Jesus' beauty makes other things less pleasing: "If the eye could have seen his glory, glory of the only begottten who proceeds from the Father, it would not wish to see anything else, nor the ear to hear something other than the word of life and salvation" (Origen).

Through A Dark Cloud

Facing God in this manner, that is by being before his greatness, is not always an easy and immediately satisfying undertaking; for at times, there seems to be a scarcely penetrable wall between us. He remains hidden behind this, which is often described by spiritual writers as a dark cloud or in the night of his unknowableness. Yet contact has to be made and maintained with him, even though he is distant behind a mysterious barrier. A mediaeval writer has wisely written about what then is called for. "It is love, in fact, that can lead to God in this life, not knowledge". Expressions of that same on our part touch him. An earlier Father already noted: "Only wonder can reach his unapproachable power" (Maximus the Confessor).

The spiritual lover struggles, in that obscure world of, to an extent, blocked spiritual horizon, seeking the Almighty. Gregory of Nyssa describes the scene: "The bride (the one searching) speaks: 'In the night I searched to know what is his essence. ... But I could not find. I called him by all the names with which one can call, but no name could reach him. How can he be reached by name – he who is beyond every name? For how can that which is always beyond everything we know be designated by a name?'". Yet such appellations are not purely useless. "The bride understands every function of a name as a sign of the ineffable good, even if the significance of each word falls short and shows something inferior to the truth". The names of God are symbols of him. The ones given to us in the Bible have to be respected and used, in order to enter correctly into his mystery! They are focuses, which concentrate on the Almighty. Through them, blind faith, spurred on by love, has communion with him.

Gregory of Nyssa lingers on this theme – that is the individual's groping for God: "For how can what is invisible be seen all right? The bridegroom bestows upon the soul a perception of his presence, although a clear apprehension escapes it since his invisible nature lies hidden. What then is the mystical initiation which the soul experiences during the night? It is the word touching the door. We understand by this door the human mind searcing for what is hidden; through it the object sought after enters. Therefore, truth stands outside our souls because, as the Apostle says (1 Cor 13.12), we know in part. Truth knocks at the mind by means of allegory and mystery saying "Open", and, with this summons, the bridegroom suggests a way we can open the door. He gives us certain keys, that is, the beautiful words of the Song. Names such as sister, companion, dove, perfect one, are clearly keys which open what is hidden" (Songs Of Songs). The response of love evoked on our side by these terms reaches the Creator. Small lights break through, as contact is made with him in his hiddenness. But alas, the more he is known, the further removed he also becomes. When peaks are reached in the ascent to him, the heights where he dwells appear all the more fearful and formidable. Yet relentlessly he draws the lover through the vague twilight to keep trying to attain him, and inspires further yearning and longing for him. While there is no end in sight, the desire can ever grow stronger to pursue him to "the mountains of myrrh and the hills of fragrance", which Origen, borrowing from the Song of Songs, says is the place where he dwells.

Purification

The person who endeavours to pierce through the wall of separation is best able to do so with a soul that is already purified. For this reason the first step towards communion with God is repentance – freeing oneself from all that sullies or stains. In Pauline terminology, the old man has to be cast off, as a condition for being clothed with the new. Only the soul without sin can enter the chamber of the bridegroom, and dwell comfortably and chastely there. Gregory of Nyssa makes clear what is called for: "Enter the inner chamber of the chaste bridegroom and clothe yourselves with the white garments of pure, chaste thoughts. Let no one bring passionate, fleshy thoughts or a garment of conscience unsuitable for divine nuptials. Let no one be bound up in his own thoughts, or drag the pure words of the bridegroom and the bride down into earthly, irrational passions" (Comm on Song of Songs). The spiritually clean have the capacity to be open to the rays of the divine splendour and the shafts of his love. "Purity of all kinds means that the soul is unsullied before God and so is transparent before him or ready to reflect his glory and brilliance. It is open to receive his graces". Another important gift is required from on high, which gives the soul the capability to be attuned to the Almighty: "In fact it is impossible to see and recognize how great is the magnificence of the word, if one has not received first the eyes of a dove, that is spiritual comprehension" (Origen). The inner eyes have to be especially sharpened, to grasp divine wisdom and mystery.

Meditating On God's Word

The incarnation or the Son of God's presence on earth made prayer in one sense less solemn and more human! Jesus is the revelation of the Father – being God living on earth as a man. He reveals in a human way the Creator, and his thinking and acting. As a result, the NT (but also the OT) abounds in much divine wisdom. Pondering over their scenes, in an effort to meet the Almighty, is prayer at its best, since it means receiving and entering into what is revealed. The Son of God is met mainly in the NT, as he walks about, converses with others, teaches, heals, and in the end suffers greatly. He appears to be just human, but is ever more than that.

The earthly Christ is also divine. Even though we encounter him in prayer as someone like ourselves "in all things but sin" (Heb 4.15), his loftiness and mystery are there too – though veiled from us. When meditating on the Gospels and seeing the human Jesus, his divine reality must be kept in mind. So the mystical approach is still valid, since his sublime greatness has to be somehow encountered.

While trying to meet the Son of God profoundly and thoroughly through the words of the NT, it is useful to consider what Gregory of Nyssa says about contemplating the words of the *Song of Songs* which he compares to a journey by sea. "The vast sea represents contemplation of the divine words. From this voyage we expect great wealth. The Church is this living vessel which expects the riches of divine guidance in all its fullness. But the Song's text, acting as pilot, does not touch the tiller before prayer is offered to God by the entire crew so that the Holy Spirit's power might breathe on us and put into action the waves of our thoughts. In this way he guides our prayer as one directs a voyage". The travel that can be made through the Bible is a long, even immense one. The Spirit needs to sharpen our minds and awaken our hearts, so that we now can draw profoundly and extensively from God's word.

Any text chosen for prayer has to be read over many times. It is a considerable help to study the writing with the aid of a commentary – one good one – while not jumping from one book to another! The reading has to be allowed to speak to us, in its own mysterious greatness. The words of the piece selected are, as it were, set in different colours, with some of them more pronounced or brighter or more significant than others. In any given passage certain expressions, words or sentences carry the most meaning. The key ideas and images that are highlighted in a text by its author should be eventually grasped. Or again, a section of Scripture is like a board with different lights flashing on it. The most pronounced of these have to be especially noted. With time and practice, the ability to perceive what is brightest there becomes sharper, and the profundities of divine revelation are seen to stand out, and impinge more strongly. The person, who takes portions of the Bible, particularly of the NT, is opening out to shades and aspects of God's mysteries.

Those who read and pray the Bible become spiritually alert for its depths. Very ordinary words, when Christ is their subject, may be most significant, such as "walking", "greeting", "listening", "doing", "going over to". He engages in all these activities for us, not just by accident, but because he always does what pleases his Father (Jn 5.19). When we read that "The glory of the Lord shone around them", we know that it shines around us too. Everything there is beneficial to us.

Dwelling on God's word, in this fashion, means drawing out the richness of the divine love and knowledge contained there. All Christ's sayings and actions have to be pondered over and entered into, especially his incarnation and death, as Gregory of Nyssa stresses. The two disciples on the way to Emmaus were shown how to pray – bringing other biblical texts to have a bearing on him: "And beginning with Moses and all the prophets, he interpreted to them in all the scriptures the things concerning himself" (Lk 24.27). Sections of the Bible throw light on other ones of the same book. "Meditating on the mysteries of Christ's life, with emphasis more on the divinity than on the humanity, adorns the soul with the divine treasures that he offers" (G. of Nyssa). Such prayer enhances the soul greatly. God has made known a vast amount about himself, whose full significance will preoccupy us for all eternity! – and in all of which we come up against his mystery.

There are dominant themes in the Bible. An awareness of these allows us to watch out for them, in different contexts. Lesser events are connected with them, and have to be drawn into them. Some of the main issues are, the Trinity, God's creation, divine generosity or love, Christ's style of life, his death and all its consequences, the role of the Spirit, Mary, the Church, and the afterlife. These classifications focus on the main presentations to us of the life and workings of God.

Scripture is read to get to know the Creator, in his greatness, goodness and originality. Each detail about the Lord there, whether a word or deed of his, has to be grasped, as far as possible, in relation to the divine fullness – God is love (1 Jn 4.7). Every expression of his is a revealed aspect of that same. Meeting him in his word is being influenced or drenched by the power of his love.

Of course prayer is not purely a matter of what happens, when this exercise is engaged in. It is a preparation for living. Its spirit has to be carried through in ordinary life, where it bears fruit in good works. It is a source from which springs sound and sane living.

Union With God

In so far as this is attained, the image of God in each person, which was darkened by sin, is restored and brightened, and the likeness to him grows. When this is adequately perfect, there is a mystical marriage between the bride (creature) and the bridegroom (Creator).

Those who attain such a union have reached the everlasting springs – to use an old image. Gregory of Nyssa writes about this: "Who can worthily comprehend the wonders applied to the Bride? It seems that she has no further to reach once she has been compared to beauty's archetype. She closely imitates her bridegroom's fountain by one of her own; his life by hers and his water by her water".

In the *Song Of Songs* the living water is said to be flowing from Lebanon – the home of the bridegroom. The bride retains the inflow of this water within the well of her own soul, and becomes a treasure house for it. All (that is those who can be classed as a bride) become partakers of God, possessing to a degree that fountain. Then as the Book of Proverbs states (5.17-18), they may drink their own water – their own inner wisdom, and not that from another well. Gregory adds that this is done in Christ Jesus our Lord, to whom be glory forever and ever. Amen. Union with God means that the individual is most perfect and self-resourceful.

In The Sphere Of God

Praying signifies being attentive to the greatness of God, and all his original manifestations of it, in an open or disposed state. That means being ready to accept him, whatever way he comes and to receive from him whatever he gives or demands. It amounts to allowing his loftiness to uplift us in every way possible. When we pray, we are offering ourselves to his power and brilliance, surrendering to his divine creativity. We are then allowing his supreme originality to shape our existences.

We never pray alone. When we turn to the Father, Christ, the Spirit, our Lady and the saints are always with us. They add force and volume to our feeble efforts to speak to or to communicate with him, and make them more effective and pleasing. When we perform this worthy exercise, we are in the heavenly sphere. To pray means to be partly in heaven!

The ways of the Almighty are strange, but they all are in every sense paths of love. However baffling they may seem, we can be assured that the person who prays is particularly wisely directed, and bears the adornment of the divine Artist. He embellishes the life of such a faithful one with mysterious strength, wisdom and beauty. The Lord can turn around every erring way for good. Prayer brings countless blessings.

15

Love And Sex

To deal with sex adequately, straightaway its positive side has to be fully recognized and accepted. Nowadays, most are aware of this and have no hesitation or doubt about it. The sexuality of each person provides a wonderful and marvellous outlet for expressing love – though some would add "in the right circumstances of course!" – about which there is no agreement. It is given by the Creator as a gift and for a purpose, and must be esteemed as such. As a result, some hold that it has to be used in the manner that he thinks fitting. According to them, when sex is viewed or approached in any other way, its beauty and goodness are not adequately appreciated nor affirmed. The same is true, when it is considered as something inappropriate or lowly. It should rather be lovingly regarded and nobly valued. This, however, brings the responsibility of availing of it in the correct manner.

It is impossible to do justice to the full role of sex in each life. Its unconscious effect on the human psyche is enormous. It would be incorrect to exclude its contribution to the artistic development of individuals! Its stimulus is latently present in all human achieving and altruistic activity! Its force is very great. Yet its role is usually viewed as much more ordinary.

True To Self

The majority wish to lead a normal life, and that means a sexual one. They want to live as they are in the real world, and not be curtailed or restrained by any visionary or lofty outlook. They have no desire to flee from sex or to suppress its existence in them. They are realistic about their make-up, even if they are to an extent reserved about it. They vividly realize that any denial of such a reality would have damaging consequences for them. The Church, as many so well know, can easily take an over-spiritual view of the human person. She "has the tendency to misunderstand bodily fruitfulness, and to see fruitfulness only in the spirit" – a past attitude at least, which Adrienne von Speyr, to take one important writer, rightly frowns on. Clearly authentic living demands having an honest appraisal of the sexual role. Its impact for good on the human person has to be willingly acknowledged and adjusted to.

Purely Natural

Many, if not the majority, view sex in a purely natural way, and even hold that nothing more should be said about it. Sexual behaviour, according to this outlook, is the fulfilment of a human need or craving – the release of naturally pent-up tension. When hunger for it is felt, the required satisfaction is called for. The way to relieve its pressing insistence depends on the possibilities available. Sex is thus viewed as a biological, exercise-demanding function.

Moralists and spiritual writers, as is well noted, have a far more cautious approach to the matter, and their attitude in the modern climate is often frowned on and rejected. The Church's traditional teaching on sex is laughed out of court in many circles. The result is that it takes a strong individual to go along with it. The influence of peer groups puts great pressure on many to accept their liberal philosophy, which advocates great ordinariness about sex and pleads for casual freedom in its use. Individuals, wanting to be part of a group, may find it hard to adhere to another opinion – one that suggests control and order in sexual matters. They fear being branded as cowardly and weak, and afraid of real life. They don't want to be considered as missing out on the swing of present-day life, and, above all, they would dread being regarded by their companions as old-fashioned or out of date, and so losing personal esteem. Some sexual manuals state the same thing: "For many young people to resist against these (modern) norms is more difficult than against the prohibitions of the old kind".

To be fair, such widespread views on sex are frequently not based purely on biological needs, however important they may be. They arise too from an acute longing felt by many for friendship and warm companionship. The sexual drive urges people to seek this, and as a result they feel wanted and appreciated. The great interest in this human force springs from several emotional factors.

Those who view the matter in a different manner are aware of how much they are at variance with the liberal view mentioned above. Adrienne von Speyr has pointed out, in her sobering and profound book, *Theology Of Sex*, that "when an individual's thinking and action start from the natural outlook, it is difficult to uplift them to a more exalted one". She adds: "And when the first experiences … take place at this level, it is difficult to raise them (subsequent ones) to a higher plane". There are clearly two very varied approaches to sex.

A Wider View

What so far has been said about it deals with the matter in general and in isolation. More particularly, there are often problems and difficulties, sometimes very painful ones, associated with it, and these can't be ignored. They are of various kinds: sexually transmitted diseases, some of which are very serious, unwanted pregnancies with all their consequences, dire abortions, abuse of people, disloyalty, terrible revenge, anxiety, hatred. Unwholesome living situations in marriage must also be included.

When the flesh or sex is too dominant in a person's life, other dimensions tend to suffer. It is not surprising then that some give up the practice of their religion, when their sexual living goes astray! Adverse situations arising from the sexual sphere (though they may have other causes too) are often expounded in newspapers and magazines. Those who work with people know how distressing these difficulties can be.

Some maintain, nevertheless, that the negative side of sex should not be dwelt on too much, as it leads to an altogether wrong attitude towards it. Its positive value should rather be concentrated on. These wish above all to avoid having an absolute outlook on it – especially in view of the pressures that have a bearing on people's lives. They accept as valid different types of relationships, transitory and more permanent ones, and are not condemnatory of the use of sex in any of these. Many often consider it as fitting in friendship, if a pair want it so. Should that love wane with time, they are willing to calmly move away – perhaps to another partner. They may eventually dedicate themselves to just one person, if life brings them to it.

In The Fullness Of Love

These who view people in their totality are wary of any partial approach to sex. They are aware that there is a tendency in all to try to separate it from love and to make it autonomous – something they regard as flawed. Each person is a unity and every action in some way involves that completeness. Sexual expression has to be in harmony with the total individual. There is something inadequate and frustrating in it, when it is otherwise experienced! After such sexual activity, neglected issues may claim consideration – causing perhaps regret and unease. When sex becomes a value in itself, divorced from a fitting human backup, it does not fit in to authentic living! A brief sexual encounter is too passing in its benefits! With time it may be seen to have been an error. The realization that sex has to be strongly rooted in true love even comes home to many, through trial and error.

Glamorizing Sex

Nowadays this is deliberately made to appear very glamorous, in advertising and colourful magazines. There beautiful bodies are portrayed in slick posing, often with scant clothing and prominent contours. Sex is presented as the key to a world of magic. But, alas, the focus is on outward adornment, as only embellished and decked out aspects of a personality are displayed. The full reality of any definite person is not given. Nothing is revealed about the character of such people, their education, qualities, ideals, beliefs, and above all about their defects. These pictures belong to the world of fancy or dreams – yet they prove very appealing! We all tend to be deceived by outward appearances! – a hazard that the Bible warns us about.

The natural beauty of a woman (and of a man too!) can lead people astray – and so Scripture advises: "Do not be ensnared by a woman's beauty" (Sir 25.20). That attraction can bring about erroneous behaviour, and no wonder the suggestion has to be made: "Turn away your eyes from a shapely woman, and do not look intently at beauty belonging to another; many have been misled by a woman's beauty, and by it passion is kindled like a fire" (Sir 9.8. Two well-known realities are a threat to sound living. "Wine and women lead intelligent men astray, and the man who consorts with harlots is very reckless" (Sir 19.2).

Individuals should not be evaluated simply by their appearance: "Do not praise a man for his good looks, nor loathe a man because of his appearance" (Sir 11.2). It's foolish to give prime importance to what is outward and external. Wasn't the Trojan war of old fought over the beauty of a woman! – a madness that the dramatist, Euripides, wisely noted. The adulteress or prostitute may display great charm, but it is far from genuine: "For the lips of a loose woman drip honey, and her speech is smoother than oil; but in the end she is bitter wormwood, sharp as a two-edged sword" (Prov 5.3,4). This is a lesson hard to learn, as the appeal of outward good looks can be very seductive!

A Religious Viewpoint

The Catholic teaching on sex – other Christians may have different views – is based mainly on the God-given vocation to each, namely to conform to his love and plan for all, which is to grow into the fullness of Christ. Sex is, thus, fittingly used, when it contributes to the scope that the Creator has set for each. It has to serve in building up fully developed and spiritual beings.

St Paul reminds us to ever keep firmly in mind our basic vocation, and that sex has to be subordinate to this: "For this is the will of God, your sanctification: that you abstain from unchastity. ... For God has not called you for uncleanness, but in holiness" (1Thess 4. 3,7). He demands an incarnated faith – one lived out bodily too. "The body is not meant for immorality, but for the Lord, and the Lord for the body. ... Do you not know that your bodies are members of Christ? Shall I therefore take the members of Christ and make them members of a prostitute. ... But whoever is joined to the Lord becomes one spirit with him" (1 Cor 6.13,15,17). The human body must ever be spiritually pleasing to the Lord.

The Christian is transformed by Christ, and his power, active in each, strives to gain control over carnal urgings: "But put you on the Lord Jesus Christ and make no provision for the desires of the flesh" (Rom 13.14. All should offer their bodies in a sacrificial state to God: "I urge you, therefore, brothers, by the mercies of God, to offer your bodies as a living sacrifice, holy and pleasing to God, your spiritual worship" (Rom 12.1). The body should give silent and dignified adoration to the Creator, by being holy. Peter indicates that God's will and not sexual drives is to be followed – "so as to live for the rest of the time in the flesh no longer by human passions, but by the will of God" (1 Pet 4.2).

Such thinking follows from the fact that the Son of God died for all, in order to save and ultimately bring them to glory. Redemption means that the whole person, body and soul, can and must be sanctified – that is made completely subject to Christ. What pertains to human sexuality has to be one stream or current in a total movement to him. Adrienne von Speyr rightly writes that all sexual matters or questions about it must be considered "not in the isolation of the sexual sphere, where there is no solution to them, but in their integration into the sphere of the whole man, the Christian, living in the Church, in Christ and in the Trinity". If sex is being lived and dealt with solely on the sensitive, pleasurable level, where there is no substitute for it, its worth is beyond question. But is it fitting to take such a limited view of it? If it is valued only for the pleasure it gives, without taking into account its other effects, is it not being assessed solely for a brief time and out of context! Sexual activity, according to Catholic teaching, has to be in tune with other human drives – tendencies, talents, and interests. It must play its part in the development of a healthy, balanced, achieving and spiritual person – to the extent that God's will permits this. It is then only by looking at a person's whole life, that its place can be ascertained properly.

Sublime Teaching, But

The Christian teaching on sex seems to many to be far too angelic. Its view that sexual activity outside a proper marriage is always wrong may be ignored by the majority, yet a minority see it as advocating sound conduct, and as ultimately divinely inspired teaching. The Church regards the liberal approach as lessening the genuineness of people, making them personally scattered and less loyal and committed to the Creator and others. Married love, in the Catholic outlook, calls for fidelity for life – so divorce is inappropriate. The sacramental pledge given brings God in, binding irrevocably a pair, and "what God has joined together, no human being must separate" (Mt 19.6). This marriage bond is both deep and total, and contains an element that can't be broken. It ought to reflect the fidelity of Christ to his Church, which embraces all and excludes no one. (Artificial contraception means blocking such universality!) Private or personal sex is regarded as egoistic, since it is self-centred and not in any way sharing.

The Church strongly proclaims her teaching, but she does not impose it on anyone – though, alas, in the past this may have happened. She tries to persuade people to accept what she considers good for them, but ultimately each individual has to choose freely whether to agree with it or not.

Many claim that such teaching is totally unreal for our present-day world. They firmly reject it, and do not even deem it worthy of consideration. For them, a satisfactory sexual life demands that they be free to arrange things as best they can. Above all, they don't want to be tied up by fixed, inflexible rules. They desire to work things out for themselves, in a way that suits them. Others are led to such an outlook by circumstances. Life, at times, puts pressure on people to abandon lofty ideas. For example, there are many lonely individuals, who find they can't survive, with any ease, in isolation, and have to make an accommodation with another person, in order to remain sane. Their choice may be frowned on as unorthodox by the Church. Others fall into similar situations, because they are weak and confused, and need personal support. Many of these find it hard to practice their religion, since they suffer a sense of guilt – a feeling that they are basically wrong. They may readily condemn themselves too much!

The drama between the flesh and the Spirit, or between religious wisdom and a purely practical view of things is as old as humanity. And it's likely to remain as long as our world lasts.

Celibacy

The Church has always set great value on the celibate way of life, esteeming highly the fruitfulness it brings about. It means handing over one's sexuality together with one's full self to God, so that he can use it totally in whatever way he wishes. The celibate becomes like a musical instrument in the Creator's hand, on whom a divinely composed melody is played out. It is, when faithfully lived by, a jewel in the Church.

But nowadays, as we are well aware, a dark shadow has been cast over such a choice, and in particular about its observance. A person chooses this way of life with a degree of blindness, but one brought about by the brightness of a vision, which has to be always preserved! As Romano Guardini pointed out, an individual may take a decision while young, which later in life could not be made so easily. Many seem to have opted for celibacy without adequately knowing themselves or having a marked calling! The result has been that their lives have become a psychological mess. Yet God works in strange ways. They may achieve great sanctity through their blundering and repentance. Failures need not cause surprise, in any walk of life!

However, the dark side of the picture does not completely destroy the positive one. Some do integrate their celibacy in a remarkably admirable way. Still celibates should not be too loftily exalted in others' thinking – when their lives may involve obvious human struggles. A realistic approach to them has to be maintained. They are not confirmed saints, and need the sacrament of confession or reconciliation as much as anyone else. Their sexual deviations, when they exist, as those of the laity, should normally be dealt with there, and not in the media!

Mystery

There is mystery involved in sex, as there is in the whole human make-up. The basic one, in the sexual sphere, is the difference between male and female. One wonders what there is in God which corresponds to each of these! This element (of mystery) can't properly be left out and has to be attended to, in all discussions on the role of man and woman.

The real value of sexual uprightness or purity is that it makes a person transparent before the Creator and more receptive of his power. Sex should never be used except when anchored in his love – poured out into each heart. It should be freeing and enriching, and not be a burden or ruining. The way forward for all is that of Christ, which is ever an ordered one. The forceful sexual drive can easily lead to activity, incompatible with the uprightness and sureness that marks the Lord's path. However, sexual errors are inevitable. Thankfully God's love is never far from the sinner, and his mercy can cope with any situation.

There is another aspect to the mystery of sex, which needs to be dwelt on. Sexual activity, as lived in the present, does not exist in the next life, where all are alive for eternity and where there is no end. It came into the world along with death, after Adam and Eve's fall. It only has a purpose and meaning in a world where people die! Sexual behaviour, then, is always an affirmation of death! It ensures that people exist who are destined to die. An over emphasis on it, regarding it as what is most worthwhile in life, is a desire to make this place the everlasting abode! It is a plea to have a fallen world supreme! This view of sex may appear too gloomy to many, but, perhaps, it deserves more study!

16

Love and Suffering

There is no need to pretend that the connection between these two is obvious or easy to grasp. If anything seems to be the opposite to love, it is suffering! It is difficult to tell those who are in turmoil and pain, particularly if it is grave, that their ailment is a blessing and should be cherished as such. Many, nevertheless, have to struggle through life, trying to find a solution to this apparent contradiction.

The extent and severity of suffering are well-known and need not be elaborated on in any descriptive manner here. We ourselves may have our own share of affliction and be vividly aware of the discomfort it causes. And yet however awful a burden it may be, we have at least a vague notion that there are blessings attached to it.

Biblical Moanings On Distress

The Bible draws our attention to the harshness of ailments and the depths of the misery they cause. The psalmist needs to lament, when speaking to God: "For thy arrows have sunk into me, and thy hand has come down on me" (Ps 38.2). It is further disturbing for him to bear in mind that his own sin brought about such acute pain: "For we are consumed by thy anger; by thy wrath we are overwhelmed. Thou hast set our iniquities before thee, our secret sins in the light of thy countenance" (Ps 90.5-6). The woes resulting from sin can be very stressful: "My wounds grow foul and fester because of my foolishness, I am utterly bowed down and prostrate; all the day long I go about mourning. For my loins are filled with burning, and there is no soundness in my flesh. I am utterly spent and crushed; I moan because of the tumult of my heart. ... My heart throbs, my strength fails me; and the light of my eyes – it also has gone from me" (Ps 38.5-8;10). Numerous other texts, showing people in grim and excruciating anguish, could be cited.

The *Book Of Job* vividly describes the horrors of the just one suffering, who has to say: "I loathe my life" (10.1). There was no sin in his case. The

Book of Revelation, through its images and horror scenes, alerts us to the plagues and violent aggressions that assail humanity, even on a cosmic scale. God allows the devil and his partners great scope, to torture and destroy many people and much of the world! They are able to open up a horrifying abyss of wickedness. If God permits this to happen, we may wonder why it is so. Where is the God of love? However, the same book stresses the victory that Christ has already won over all such forces, and even hints at universal salvation! The tormentors have no control over the ultimate destiny of anyone. Suffering, however cruel and devastating, has, despite all, a fitting and mysterious place in the embrace of God's redeeming love.

A Punishment For Sin

The Bible makes several attempts to explain the riddle of human distress and offers various views as to its meaning. A very old one is that it is a punishment for sin – as in the case of Adam and Eve, on whom toil, weariness, pain and death were decreed, because they disobeyed God. Their penalty was enormous. Still, the resulting misfortunes, which affect all of us, were not merely punitive, but opened out to an intended salvation. When God punishes, he does so in order to offer a greater gift – something that is always worth remembering. Even though he castigated the first pair and all their descendants, he offered them hope, because of the wonderful solution to their woes which he had in mind. He promised to send a redeemer, to set things aright, and, as later was discovered, to display immensely his goodness. Though their suffering might be burdensome, it was imposed with a view to something extraordinary. He set their lives moving towards a newer and far better era. Without their disobedience, the divine Saviour would not have been necessary.

In view of his method of punishing, God seriously warned the Israelites how to behave. "And now, O Israel, give heed to the statutes and the ordinances which I teach you, and do them; that you may live, and go in and take possession of the land which the Lord, the God of our fathers gives you. ... Take heed to yourself, lest you forget the covenant of the Lord your God, which he made with you. ... For the Lord your God is a devouring fire, a jealous God" (Dt 4.1,23,24). There is pain in store for those who don't go God's way, unless they repent! A bad situation can be made worse by sin. "See, I have set before you this day life and good, death and evil. If you obey the commandments of the Lord your God ... then you shall live and multiply, and the Lord your God will bless you. But if your heart turns away ... I declare to you that you shall perish" (Dt 30. 15-18).

A widely held biblical outlook is that the good fare well, while things go wrong for the wicked. The bad bring misfortune upon themselves, while fortune favours the upright. "Misfortune pursues sinners" (Pr 13.21). "In all that he (the good) does (she too), he prospers ... but the way of the wicked will perish" (Ps 1.3-4). Goodness directs individuals wisely along, while evil is harmful. "The integrity of the upright guides them, but the crookedness of the treacherous destroys them" (Pr 2.6). "An evil man is ensnared in his transgression, but the righteous man sings and rejoices" (Pr 29.6). The length of a person's life is dependent on good conduct: "The fear of the Lord prolongs life, but the years of the wicked will be short" (Pr 10.27).

Suffering is thus regarded, in this outlook, as following automatically wrongdoing, or is planned by God's providence to strike after it. The prophets can correctly foretell that destruction and sorrow are in store for the chosen people, because they continue on sinning. "Their tongue is a deadly arrow; it speaks deceitfully. ... Shall I not punish them for these things? says the Lord" (Jer 9.8-9). The travail of the land and its inhabitants are due to their wickedness: "There is no faithfulness, and no knowledge of God in the land. ... Therefore the land mourns, and all who dwell in it languish" (Hos 4.1,3). The Almighty cannot ignore those who gaily go on sinning, heaping wickedness on wickedness, but has to try to curb them: "How can I pardon you? Your children have forsaken me, and have sworn by those who are not gods. When I fed them to the full, they committed adultery, and trooped to the houses of harlots. They were well-fed lusty stallions, each neighing for his neighbours wife. Shall I not punish them for these things, says the Lord; and shall I not avenge myself on a nation such as this?" (Jer 5.7-9).

The prodigal son must have realized that the dire circumstance he found himself in was a punishment for his sins. "A great famine arose in that country, and he began to be in want" (Lk 15.14). Jesus recognized the existence of such punishment, when he said to the man whom he cured at the pool of Bethsaida: "Sin no more that nothing worse befall you" (Jn 5.14). However, this outlook is never a complete one, as Jesus says: "It was not that this (blind) man sinned or his parents" (Jn 9.3). Suffering does not always point to previous sins.

A Call To Repentance And Educative

When the Almighty acts in a reactionary role, his concern is never just to punish, but also to correct the erring person – and all is governed by love. "Those whom I love, I reprove and chasten; so be zealous and repent" (Rev 3.19). He has in mind their sanctification: "He disciplines us for our good that we may share in his holiness" (Heb 12.10). The Lord's intolerance of sin causes him to do something about it – which can only be to correct the sinner.

Suffering is a call to repentance – to look towards a more pleasing side of the Almighty. "Return to the Lord, your God, for he is gracious and merciful, slow to anger and abounding in steadfast love" (Joel 2.13). The sinner has benefited from his suffering, when he prays: "For I am ready to fall, and my pain is ever with me. I confess my iniquity, I am sorry for my sin. ... Make haste to help me, O Lord, my salvation" (Ps 38.17, 18, 22). The Lord's anger lasts only for a time (Ps 30.5). Any pain he causes is a divine effort to help and to be generous.

Such correction needs to be lovingly accepted. "My son, do not despise the Lord's discipline or be weary of his reproof, for the Lord reproves him whom he loves, as a father the son in whom he delights" (Prov 3.11, 12). Suffering is brought about by divine love – though it may have other causes. "Know then in your heart that, as a man disciplines his son, the Lord your God disciplines you" (Dt 8.5).

However purposeful it may be, such hardship can be severe and pro-longed: "Man is also chastened with pain upon his bed and with continual strife in his bones" (Jb 33.19). Yet this is only one side of the matter. There are blessings attached to it too. "Behold, happy is the man whom God reproves; therefore despise not the chastening of the Almighty. For he wounds, but he binds up, he smites, but his hands heal" (Jb 5. 17-18).

Suffering viewed in this manner is always educative. The Greek drama-tist, Aeschylus, stressed this, saying: "By suffering, we learn". Not only does it enable us to have sympathy for others in distress, but it helps us to acquire many virtues, as St. Paul says: "We rejoice in our sufferings, knowing that suffering produces endurance, and endurance produces char-acter, and character produces hope" (Rom 5. 3-4).

Each of us has to try to discover the religious meaning of our own suf-fering. We are never wrong, when we conclude that it is a reminder to us to live more correctly and to seek God's help. "My son, when you are ill, delay not, but pray to God who will heal you: Flee wickedness; let your hands be just, cleanse your heart of every sin" (Sir 38.9-10). However, neither this viewpoint given here nor others can fully explain the signifi-cance of pain. It is always part of the mystery of God's love for us, which is beyond our complete understanding, and which has to be accepted in a humble spirit of trust.

A Trial

It is tempting to consider God at times as daring – exposing people to much risk and even failure, when he sets trials before them. Yet he knows all individually, and is aware of what they, with his help, can withstand. The hardships which they have to face enable them to assert the genuineness of their goodness, and even to extend it, by rising to greater nobility. By cling-ing firmly to God with respect and trust, in spite of disappointment, dis-tress, failure or pain, the strength of an individual's belief is affirmed. Under the pressure of suffering, the real fibre of each person is known.

With this in mind, God tested the Israelites in the desert, so that they could confirm their loyalty to him: "And you shall remember all the ways which the Lord your God has led you these forty years in the wilderness, that he might humble you, testing you to know what was in your heart, whether you would keep his commandments or not" (Dt 8.2). The Israelites found the going remarkably tough there, and did not readily trust in nor obey the Lord. Their journey in the wilderness was a severe test for them. Those who inflict pain on the just, according to the *Book Of Wisdom* know that, at the same time, they are setting a trial before them. They say: "Let us test him with insult and torture that we may find out how gentle he is, and make trial of his forbearance" (Ws 2.19).

The tests that God assails us with can be very severe. They can shatter our lives so much, that we may feel that we can't continue on, without a breakdown. Abraham, noted for the many trials he had to endure, must have been in a similar situation, when God asked him to sacrifice his only and difficultly-acquired son – his pride and joy, he on whom rested his hopes. And yet, with steadfast resolve and perhaps trembling feet, he obeyed. In doing so, he was in touch with and surrendering to the myste-rious side of the Creator – an aspect of him that he did not know. God's glory was shining on him with an intensity that he could scarcely bear; still it seemed only darkness to him. He bowed to what the Lord wanted, recognizing it as more important than all that was dear to him. It was the hardest ordeal that he could have been asked to undertake! He must have questioned in his numbness why the Almighty wanted so much of him, but still he obeyed.

In the case of Job, all that is humanly attractive in life, his family, pos-sessions, and his own comfort are taken away from him. Addressing God he asks: "Does it seem good to thee to oppress, to despise the work of thy hands and favour the designs of the wicked?" (10.3). Every effort he makes to come to terms with his lot, only makes his situation worse: "And if I lift myself up, thou dost hunt me like a lion, and again work wonders against me" (10.16). God appears to be silent and distant, leaving him unanswered in the abyss of his torment and bewilderment.

Nothing much more is left to him than his consciousness of distress and its puzzling meaning for him. Those who try to make him face the root cause of his situation are not up to the task, but nevertheless they don't hesitate to convey their thinking – (How often does this happen in life!). His pain, groans, sighs and lack of understanding are a lamentation directed to God. In the end, the light of further revelation breaks through. Pain is the language that can lead to a higher knowledge of and meeting with God. Through the torment, bewilderment and darkness of his suffering, Job is exposed to another side of the Almighty – to a wisdom and goodness that for a time hide their value. The more puzzled he becomes, the richer is his veiled contact with the greatness of the Lord. God is creatively and lovingly at work, even when people struggle in a whirlwind of torment, and don't find meaning in it. "The crucible is for silver and the furnace is for gold, and the Lord tries hearts" (Pr 17.3).

The suffering servant (a figure that anticipates Christ), as described by the second Isaiah, was severely tested with harsh treatment – all for the sins of others. He was reduced to a state, in which he, in no way, appeared attractive. "He had no form or comeliness that we should look at him, and no beauty that we should desire him. He was despised and rejected by men; a man of sorrows and acquainted with grief" (Is 53.2-3). Still it was all for a noble purpose: "He was wounded for our transgressions, he was bruised for our iniquities" (53. 5). "The lord has laid on him the iniquity of us all" (53.6). "It was the will of the Lord to bruise him; he has put him to grief; when he makes himself an offering for sin" (53.10). He himself had done no harm (53.9). But very generously, he went serenely through it all. "Like a lamb that is led to the slaughter, and like a sheep that before its shearers is dumb, so he opened not his mouth" (Is 53.7). He must have realized that such sufferings would be of great benefit to others. This is an important fact: all pain is not purely personal, but overflows in its worth to others. The suffering servant is a universal benefactor.

Jesus' sufferings were also a trial. The NT speaks of his endurance – "Who for the joy that was set before him endured the cross" (Heb 12.2). His death, brought about by cruel torture, tested his obedience and love. But this brings him closer to all others. "For because he himself has suffered and being tempted, he is able to help those who are tempted" (Heb 2.18). A great mystery is involved in this ordeal, succinctly put in the Epistle to the Hebrews: "Although he was a Son (God's unique and only one), he learned obedience through what he suffered" (Heb 5.8). The two levels in his life are held together in some mysterious way, without in any way diminishing his humanity. No one can ever claim that Jesus had it easy. The genuineness of faith and love, in any one, only comes to the fore through testing. "In this you rejoice, though now for a little while you may have to suffer various trials, so that the genuineness of your faith, more precious than gold which though perishable is tested by fire, may redound to praise and glory and honour at the revelation of Jesus Christ" (1 P 1.7).

Even when suffering is a trial, it is never purely so. It involves a process of growth, of refinement and giving way to the Almighty. "The testing of your faith produces steadfastness" (Jm 1.3). It leads to wisdom – to being near to the Creator. "She(wisdom) walks with him as a stranger, and at first she puts him to the test; Fear and dread she brings upon him and tries him with her discipline; With her precepts she puts him to the proof, until his heart is fully with her" (Sir 4.17). Suffering draws all to the Lord. Christ's endurance brought him far. He was "crowned with glory and honour because of the suffering of death" (Heb 2.9).

Suffering As Redemptive And Sanctifying

Jesus' pain wasn't mainly a test, but had another more important purpose – it was redemptive. It is his passion which best reveals the mystery of suffering to us, and it is something that we should ever try to learn from. His excruciating ordeal, brought about by cruel torture, shows his incalculable generosity. He did not suffer for himself, but for others. "Christ died for us" (Rom 5.8). He carried all our ills and ailments on the cross. "He himself bore our sins in his body on the tree" (1 Pet 2.24). "He took our iniquities and bore our diseases" (Mt 8.17). Our sins caused his death: "Jesus was put to death for our trespasses and raised for our justification" (Rm 4.25). "And he died for all, that those who live might live no longer for themselves but for him who for their sake died and was raised" (2 Cor 5.15). He underwent the grimmest of all happenings, to free all from sin and to enable them to share in the divine life. His suffering was the birth pangs that brought about a redeemed world. The turmoil he went through achieved enormously. The manner in which he endured is also extraordinarily impressive. His words on the cross reveal his calm and dignified grandeur.

All our suffering is included in his pain. It identifies us to an extent with Christ on the cross and with his saving work. Those who realize this connection know that what they have to endure not only ennobles them, but is also helpful to others. The suffering are great benefactors! Their pain makes them very generous.

After receiving the Holy Spirit, Jesus' disciples were glad to be able to share in his trials. Though they were beaten and commanded not to preach about Jesus, "they left the presence of the council, rejoicing that they were counted worthy to suffer dishonour for the name" (Acts 5.41). Paul is aware that the power of the resurrection flows from his personal discomfort, and that he is "always carrying in the body the death of Jesus, so that the life of Jesus may also be manifested in our bodies" (2 Cor 4.10). He rejoices in his sufferings, seeing them as a necessary prolongation of those of Christ: "Now I rejoice in my sufferings for your sake, and in my flesh I complete what is lacking in Christ's afflictions for the sake of his body, that is, the Church" (Col 1.24). Peter recognizes what he has to endure as part of the Christian calling: "For Christ also suffered for you, leaving you an example, that you should follow in his steps" (1 P 2.21). Pain and aches, then, have to be looked at by the Christian as necessary and fitting. We should vividly realize that our distress and burdens, which weigh us down and leave us dispirited and moody, have a deeper and very positive significance. They blend in with Christ's horrific pain on the cross, and pave the way for our resurrection with him.

The Deeper Mystery

The idea of suffering leads us further into the mystery of the Trinity. Christ's own pain has in some sense existed from all eternity. It is included – though not physically – in his total self-giving to the Father. There is some element there which fully corresponds with what he later had to endure. Suffering, then, has a part of God's life.

In line with this, it would be wrong to presume that the Father and the Holy Spirit were untouched by the sufferings of Jesus on the cross. Not to be moved in some way, while others are in distress, is hardly the mark of true love! Furthermore, it would seem odd that God is not preoccupied and disturbed by the persistent sin and corruption of this world! Likewise, we should not exclude a rightful melancholic element – often a stimulant to creativity – from his love! The blessings that can derive from suffering, as we know it – opening us out to God and others – may ever be needed, and may result from another type of it, a painless one! It is a contributing factor to great nobility.

It is useful for us to bear in mind that we don't fully understand the richness of suffering. We rather consider it as part of being poor and miserable.

In The Light Of Love

However much we suffer, through our own fault or not, all is governed by Christ's mysterious love. By means of it, Jesus leads us to be like himself, in his great generosity, and also to enter more deeply into the life of the Blessed Trinity. It is a strange reality, as we experience it now – a part of a world of sin. But it seems to have richer and nobler aspects! Who can claim to see wisely its whole scenario, especially in its detail!

Death and Beyond in the Context of Love

The greatest enemy of earthly love, from a human point of view, is death. No matter how precious and beautiful a loving relationship may be, sooner or later it has to end. The eternal Reaper never fails at his task, and can quickly grasp his shears and tear asunder a happy bond of love. God shows, whenever he wishes, his mastery over life and death. He has the hour of the departure of each one fixed – and there is no escape from it. "There is an appointed time for everything. ... A time to be born and a time to die" (Ecles 3.1-2). "It is appointed that human beings die once, and after this the judgement" (Heb 9.27). Death makes very clear that God is in control.

The Seeming End

A dead person or corpse offers no sign of life, portraying a marble-like stiffness and paleness. A lifeless body gives no indication that much more should be said about it. The whole bodily machinery has ceased to function. The only possibility of movement arises from the total passivity of the dead one – whose body can be moved around for a time. A more lasting law, however, is prevailing: "Unto dust you shall return". The only way forward, according to the most obvious point of view, is downwards.

The dead one seems to have completely departed, and will never be the same again. No longer can such a one be seen, with previously known gait and comportment. A characteristic way of walking or speaking or laughing won't be noticed any more. Stories often told and good humour displayed and appreciated are forever silent. Direct communication with the deceased has ceased to be feasible. How often do questions flash across our minds, which we would love to put to departed ones, but can't, alas, do so! There is no choice but to recognize the wall of silence and invisibility that separates those that have gone from us – and to be content to live in the poverty of their absence.

While gazing at a corpse or pondering on a dead person, we have to turn to God, to find light and vision in the face of the darkness of the mystery of death. Our faith assures us that the seeming inertia there before us hides the true reality. The abyss of earthly decay is brightened over by the hidden light of God's sway, and an image of desolation can be regarded as flourishing, due to the splendour of the almighty Artist. Faith, in the face of death, makes what seems static mobile – what is lost found. Belief puts an earthly demise in an altogether different perspective.

Death Something Inevitable

Revelation tells us that death came into the world as a result of Adam and Eve's sin. It is the final punishment for humanity, which the Creator saw fitting, after the first pair refused to recognize God's lordship, and disobeyed him. They were banned from the garden of Eden (Gen 3.24), and there was no getting back there – neither for themselves nor for their descendants. Death is part of the life that is lived outside the former privileged place. It is an inevitable consequence of sin and of an existence lived in turmoil – which wears all down and weakens them! The connection between evil and mortality has to be acknowledged – even if we don't clearly and fully know the link between them. Yet death, considered in the light of what it leads to, means that the punishment it inflicts is limited.

Seeing it under this aspect is only one side of its reality. The departure of each gives great scope to the Creator's salvific power. The final exit of all is bathed in divine kindness and mercy – and is so to an enormous degree. No wonder the Bible advises us: "Fear not death's decree for you; remember it embraces those before you, and those after. Thus God has ordained for all flesh; why then should you reject the will of the Most High?" (Sir 41.3,4). Bending lovingly to it is the last act of submission to the Almighty on earth. And the ease in which it is done sums up a person's whole life! The Lord is very much involved in the demise of each one, even if there are other immediate causes. It is a creative work of his, and bears the stamp of his designing skill, which can be noted in the time, circumstances and manner of each one's farewell. No matter how grim or strange the way in which someone dies, there is more to the story than what seems. A tragedy in a human exit summons us not just to be baffled by it, but to look for and to hope in an individual mystery of divine love, played out in a bewildering fashion.

Death calls each one of us to calmly and trustingly surrender to the Lord, who meets us through it. When viewed or faced up to correctly, it has an appealing face, and its grimness vanishes – as von Balthasar so splendidly wrote: "The predatory gesture of voracious death is overcome by the gesture of surrender of the dying man (person)".

Christ The Key

Jesus holds the key to death, as he himself says: "I hold the keys of death and the underworld" (Rev 1.18). He has experienced both and gone through them, yet shaken them off in a conquering burst of energy, both taming and mastering them. He could do so because he is the resurrection and the life (Jn 11.25). He showed that he was more powerful than these seemingly destructive forces. He brings hopefully all with him, in the sweep of his rising power. "For if we believe that Jesus died and rose, so too will God through Jesus bring with him those who have fallen asleep" (1 Thess 4.14). St Paul is confident when he writes "knowing that he who raised the Lord Jesus will raise us also with Jesus and bring us with him into his presence" (2 Cor 4.14).

Death is now in a winning setting, since it "is swallowed up in victory. … But thanks be to God who gives us the victory through our Lord Jesus Christ" (1 Cor 15.55,57). He has changed the reality of our earthly end most remarkably – making it an opening out to a new and wonderful life with him. It is the doorway to an unimaginably rich existence. Christian hope looks to a bright future, and should do so confidently and without anxiety: "He (a Saviour, the Lord Jesus Christ) will change our lowly body to conform with his glorified body by the power which enables him also to bring all things into subjection to himself" (Phil 3.20). We will be greatly transformed, and have an imperishable, glorious, and spiritual body.

Faith in and devotion to Christ the conqueror of death and sin are useful and important. We should aim at dying serenely, accepting the Lord's beckoning, while yielding to the redeeming force of his power! Adam brought death, but Christ brings life: "For just as in Adam all die, so too in Christ shall all be brought to life" (1 Cor 15.22). Though we are under a sentence of death, while we are in Christ, we are in an unshakeable, living position. With him we cannot fail. The Son of God came on earth to save sinners (1 Tim 1.15), and each one of us benefits from this. He has reconciled all to himself: "Those who were once alienated and hostile in mind … he has now reconciled in his fleshy body through his death, to present you holy, without blemish, and irreproachable before him" (Ef 1.21). He has achieved an immense amount for us, for which we must be ever grateful. The more we are so, the easier will be our final departure!

Judgement

It is not so much dying, as having to appear alone before the Son of God and to give an account of our lives, which makes us fearful and alarmed about what lies ahead. Many biblical texts set a very scary scene: "We must all appear before the judgement seat of Christ, so that each one may receive good or evil, according to what he has done in the body" (2 Cor 5.10). "For he will render to every person according to his works" (Rom 2.6. Our sins make us wary of this encounter. We sense that our wickedness clings too closely to us, and that we haven't adequately shaken off our evil longings or our attraction to what is bad. We are afraid that we will have to appear before the Almighty in an ambiguous state. The realization that our sinful actions still continue on doing damage or that the harm we have done is ever negatively at work is a further disturbing factor. We don't fancy at all a clear exposure of our situation. Yet there are other mighty considerations in our favour.

There is a second set of texts in the Bible, which inspire greater hope for us. "If you, O Lord, mark iniquities, Lord, who can stand? But with you is forgiveness that you may be revered. ... For with the Lord is kindness and with him is plenteous redemption" (Ps 29.3,4,7). The might of God's eternal love far outweighs the negativity of wickedness in us. Christ is our salvation: "God made Christ our sanctification and redemption" (1 Cor 1.30). And "If God is for us, who is against us?" (Rom 8.31). The correct approach to judgement is to look to Jesus as the Saviour, saying, "You are my salvation".

It may be claiming too much to assert that the Creator can't be merciful after death. He is always gracious, with a love that is mysterious. There may be goodness in his mercy to us that we have never dreamed of. Who knows what streaks of uprightness in us, his eyes will bring to light, at the vital time of our judgement? The Christian funeral liturgy, in this regard, is very hopeful, containing a very assuring, trusting prayer: "May God give him(her) a merciful judgement". He knows our frailty. Judgement is, perhaps, best considered as the Lord bringing to light what is good in each, and so is a stepping-stone to salvation. Our sins may have vanished before this! "Christ, having been offered once to bear the sins of many, will appear a second time, not to deal with sin but to save those who are eagerly waiting for him" (Heb 9.28).

According to John's Gospel, our judgement takes place on earth, and boils down to whether we choose Christ or not: "He who believes in him (Jesus) is not condemned; he who does not believe is condemned. ... And this is the judgement, that the light has come into the world, and people loved darkness rather than light" (Jn 3.18-19). The simple prayer, perhaps only daily said, "I accept you, O Jesus, and I believe in you", will be shown later to be very salvific.

It must never be forgotten that Christ died for all sins. They are on him on the cross, and there they are burnt in the fire of divine love. With him all have died to sin – a marvellous happening which has already taken place in each person. "We are convinced that one has died for all; there-fore all have died" (2 Cor 5.14). Even the wickedness of the most mali-cious of sinners has been blotted out by Christ's redeeming work on Calvary. A desire that what he has achieved may come to the fore in an individual, at the moment of judgement, is enough to ensure salvation! Those who appeal to Christ to make his achievements vividly real in their lives can't be disappointed! The experience we have of our petitions to God being somehow answered should help us to have calm trust in him. The individual, who at the hour of death sees the Son of God raised on the cross and makes a quiet call to him for help, can hardly do so in vain! In such a setting, the cry, "Lord, be merciful to me a sinner" is claiming a gift that has already been given. In fact, this same prayer always anticipates and prepares for judgement. The one who constantly seeks God's pardon is ready for meeting the Saviour.

Devotion to our Lady is a plea to her to be with us as we die – to pre-pare us for what lies ahead and to help us to be calm and trusting. The fre-quently repeated prayer,'Pray for us sinners now and at the hour of our death' will eventually finally influence us. The saints and our dead rela-tives assist us too, as we move closely towards judgement. Prayer to the Communion of Saints makes sure that a vast host of friends are always with us.

Purgatory

This is the abode of those who, after death, are being purified and pre-pared for eternal life. To enter heaven total purity is needed. "Nothing unclean shall enter it" (Rev 21.27). The divine light must shine unsullied in each person, in order for such a one to be fit for the loftiest of dwelling places. What makes an individual unsuitable for the blessedness and nobility of on high has first to be destroyed (1 Cor 3.11-15) – happily in the fire of God's love. Such a burning was enkindled on Christ on the cross, when he took on himself the sin of the world. Purgatory is the last sharing in the redeeming sufferings of Christ!

As we appear before the splendour and uprightness of Christ in judge-ment, a spontaneous sense of unease will make it abundantly clear that we lack important personal qualities or capabilities. The degree to which we correspond to him and the extent that this is missing will become very obvious. But with this, in the kind presence of Jesus, an urgent sense of responsibility and a longing to change and better ourselves will immedi-ately be felt. We will undertake such a task with enthusiasm and zeal. It will not be a severe punishment, even if an arduous and difficult burden.

The whole process of purgatory is a training for something marvellous

– for dwelling with and seeing God. Shame for our sins and failures will have to be lived through, but availed of to acquire a profound appreciation of what is true and upright, and to lead to great integrity. Our self-esteem and hope will be enhanced, as we ever distance ourselves more from the baseness of our sins. We will be pleased that our defects are being removed by the divine and mercifully healing Lord (the spiritual Surgeon). By his wounds we will be completely healed. Our horizons will be widened, and we will become further authentic.

What basically happens is that we are being turned away from ourselves (our own "ego") – from seeing things our way, that is selfishly, to having God's outlook and his concern for others. On earth we view our sins from our own point of view, but, before God, we will become aware of their full wickedness. We have not yet sufficiently realized how much his word summons us to adjust to him and to others, nor have we allowed its inspiring and creative sparks to free and broaden us to the extent that they can. This is remedied by meditating on Christ's actions and words, especially his passion. In this way, we grow in hallowing God's name and allowing his kingdom to come in us. We become at one with divine goodness, in so far as we can – especially as manifested in Jesus' life and death.

A feeling or intuition of the better things to come – the joy that is set before us – keeps us keenly advancing. When the stage is reached in which we sense that we are as receptive of and as committed to the Creator, as we can be for now, and that the word of God has no further lights to give us in our present state, then our purgatory is over. And then it's on to eternal life.

The majority of us mortals, perhaps, pass through this cleansing and educating stay!

Hell

The prospect of eternal damnation is scarcely thinkable. And yet where else can the devil be! The thought of it is enough to provoke horror, anxiety and even despair in us. It is real for us, at least hypothetically. Whoever dies in grave sin is doomed to eternal suffering. Some may then ask, "Does this in fact happen?", and add "Hopefully it does not".

It is, nevertheless, a possibility that must seriously be reckoned with. Von Balthasar has written: "The thought of hell remains fantastic and fanciful, and cannot be taken with proper seriousness, as long as it is not given form by contrast with the love that redeemed us …; otherwise he (any sinner) can always raise some objection to the real possibility of God abandoning a person". Hell is a total rejection of God's immense love, shown in Christ's redeeming work. Turning away completely from such great mercy merits something drastic! – even as extreme and severe as hell!

Many think that accepting this belief is really a contradiction for them. They fail to square its reality with their faith in an all-loving God. How could such a Creator be so cruel as to tolerate the never ending unhappiness of a creature? Yet Christ himself wasn't spared such a grim experience – he descended into hell, being abandoned by his Father! – but it was only for a brief period.

Some put forward the view that hell means the annihilation of a person. Others avoid giving any explanation of it, holding that it is part of the mystery of iniquity or wickedness, which one just has to accept. Many rightly regard it as pertaining to the dark side of the Almighty – his mysterious sense of horror. Can we fall into this domain? Hopefully, we won't. Whatever it be, thinking on it should make us steady and alert.

If we thought too isolatedly on this subject, we could easily become spiritually crippled with fear. It is more helpful to bear in mind that between there and here, Christ stands uplifted high on the cross. Before anyone goes there, he, the Saviour, has to be pushed out of the way – something not easily done. The power flowing from his death and resurrection blocks access to such a grim underworld, unless fought fiercely against. Rather than be gloomy and sad at what might lie ahead, it would be better to look lovingly towards the dying and rising Christ, and appeal humbly for his infinite protection and mercy. "O God, be merciful to me, a sinner". His redemptive strength and goodness can snatch us all from the jaws of a final destruction, and kindly direct us to a fully satisfying abode. Faith in Christ makes us secure.

Heaven

What we hope for and aim at is to be with God in the next world. There are many biblical names for eternal life: Paradise (Lk 23.43), eating of the tree of life (Rev 2.7), being a pillar in the temple of God (Rev 3.12), the new Jerusalem (Rev 21.2), a new heaven and a new earth (Rev 21.1).

It is impossible for us to anticipatingly describe or imagine the joy that God has prepared for those who love him, since the originality of God's creativity is too mysteriously great for us. The main characteristic of heaven is briefly stated in the Bible – though that cannot be clarified much either: "Behold God's dwelling is with men (women too). He will dwell with them" (Rev 21.3) – but in such a way that they will be participating in his life. We will, hopefully, be able to know him somehow in a face to face setting, when we will be able to see and perceive him in an altogether new and wonderful way. We will be given the capacity for this beforehand. He will captivate us with his dignity and splendour. We will find the richness of his love fully absorbing and satisfying. His brilliance, in its variety and wonder, will ever stunningly win our admiration. However, these tend to be just exterior descriptions, when the afterlife consists mainly in sharing in or experiencing God's mysterious life.

Heaven is a world that is ever novel: "Behold, I make all things new" (Rev 21.3). There will be nothing stale there – nothing negative or failing. "He (God) will wipe every tear from their eyes, and there shall be no more death or mourning or pain" (Rev 21.4). So much on earth grows weary and dull with time – even friendships that once showed great sparkle and glow. But in heaven there will be continuous surprises, ever pleasantly unforeseen twists to things. The river of life-giving water is there "sparkling like crystal, flowing from the throne of God and the Lamb"'. Such water, a figure of the Holy Spirit makes all vigorous and bright. The tree of life gives abundant nourishment to each. All reign with God there – sharing in his lordship over creation. It is a land of kings or rulers, with no subjects.

Dante has written about the wonder, splendour, harmony, music and sweet smell of the eternal abode. It exceeds all that we can imagine or dream of – offering a beauty beyond colour, a sweetness of sound that no music here can vie with, a softness, taste, and smell which earthly delights cannot compare with. "Eye has not seen". It is totally different, original and marvellous.

Heaven does not mean a state of leisurely inactivity. But what has to be done there causes no weariness or frustration. God is adored, praised and appreciated – a perspective which puts lesser things in place. Perhaps Dante is right, claiming that we live in groups there, in the heavenly sphere assigned to us! We will relate mainly with these near to us, but there will be movement between the different sections – so heavenly travel! We may be sent on different missions too – to teach others our skills and insights!

What keeps the heart burning and aglow is the love which the presence of the Creator inspires, and which fills all with joy. When we gaze on him there, we will ever be drawn towards his fullness and moulded by his beauty. His brighness is most attractive, and makes all on whom it shines, glitter with soothing light. All living in heaven is marked by a super-abundance of everything, by joyful love and serenity.

Maintaining Hope

The vision of what lies ahead should leave us hopeful and not fearful. We are constantly reminded of the nearness of death, as relatives and acquaintances pass on. Such happenings smooth our final path! What they have courageously gone through should not be unduly difficult for us! We can even ask them to assist us, especially when we are approaching there.

When anguish assails us as regards our earthly departure, we need to remind ourselves that our love for God is not as bright as it should be. If we are reluctant to think so far ahead and try, as far as possible, to avoid doing so – how we cling to life down below! – we should rather seek to be more open and trusting. We have to cultivate a friendly attitude towards death.

Meanwhile it is important that we keep on course to the Father of lights, walking with and in Christ, who is the way (Jn 14.6), helped by the Holy Spirit. Our paths of life, if chosen wisely, are where the Son, the good shepherd, is leading us. When things are so, the doorway that death signifies is a bright passage for us. It offers us ultimate success. "Happy are you who fear the Lord, who walk in his ways" (Ps 128.1).

The initial stages of eternal life begin while we are on earth: "For this is eternal life to know you the one true God and Jesus Christ whom you have sent" (Jn 17.3). Being acquainted with him is the source of all true life, including the eternal one.

Epilogue

This writing has touched on many facets of love, moving far from the exuberance of a romantic scene to that shown by Christ on the cross, and to the workings of his redemptive activity. The richness and mystery of God's great love has been treated too in many places – but only to a degree. This subject is inexhaustible and mysterious. Before divine love, which is God himself, we need to bend the knee in adoration. Yet that ever expanding reality sweeps through all things, giving them life and duration – even if only a pale reflection of his.

Love may be viewed as a mighty force that has to be allowed to direct people on its own terms. Often we show resistance to this, but at our own peril. To take an example, human love is very fragile, unless it is propped up and supported by the movement or sway of divine affection. Because we are sinners, we block the onrush of God's immense love, and fail to measure up to what it demands. We tend to be afraid of genuine love.

This book is written to enable the ordinary, thoughtful person to appreciate the wonder, marvel, and scope of love. It summons all to open out to it, to embrace it with eagerness and to grow in it as far as possible. The adventure of such growth is the most exhilarating one that there is.

St. Augustine reminds us that love's priorities need to be maintained: "In some mysterious way, the man who loves himself and not God, does not truly love himself; and he truly loves himself who loves God and not himself". The Almighty is at the heart of all true love! – which is for us both a channel and power (a way, a truth, a life), transforming us and leading us to him. The greatest help we can give to others is to make them more loving.

May this book help its readers to do precisely that. May it assist them to be steeped more in love, and to have the outlook and vision that it inspires. What further can be done?

James Kelly, S.J.